Interdependence

Janet Harper

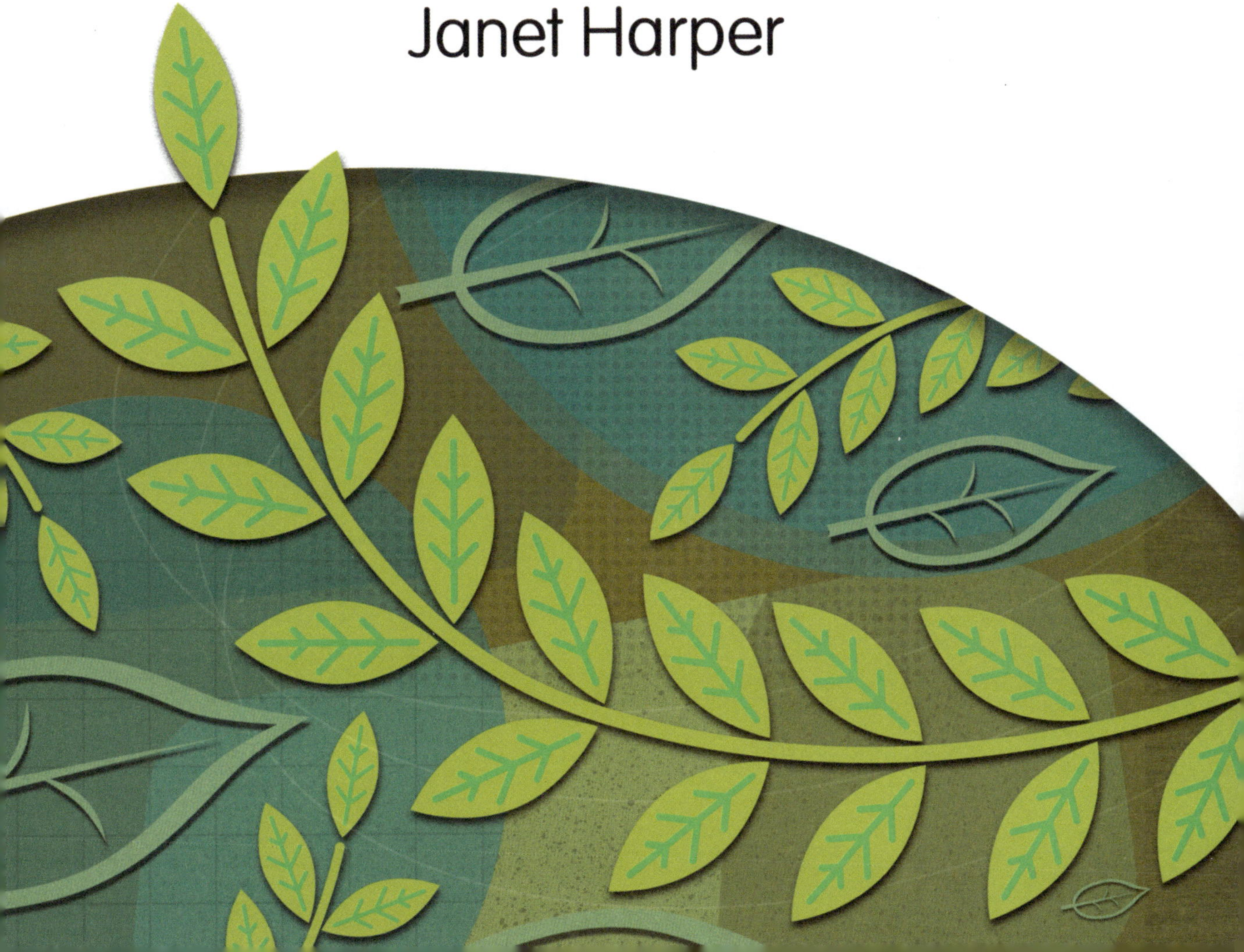

Published by Letts Educational
The Chiswick Centre
414 Chiswick High Road
London W4 5TF
Telephone: 020 89963333
Fax: 020 87428390
E-mail: mail@lettsed.co.uk
Website: www.letts-education.com

Letts Educational is part of the Granada Learning Group.

Granada Learning is a division of ITV plc.

© Janet Harper 2005

First published 2005

ISBN 1844190277

The author asserts the moral right to be identified as the author of this work.

All rights reserved. No part of this publication may be reproduced, stored in a retrieval system, or transmitted in any form or by any means, electronic, mechanical, photocopying, recording or otherwise, without either the prior permission of the Publisher or a licence permitting restricted copying in the United Kingdom issued by the Copyright Licensing Agency Ltd, 90 Tottenham Court Road, London W1P 9HE. This book is sold subject to the condition that it shall not by way of trade or otherwise be lent, hired out or otherwise circulated without the publisher's prior consent.

All web addresses are correct at the time of going to press. The information in this book has been thoroughly researched and checked for accuracy. Safety advice is given where appropriate. Neither the authors nor the publishers can accept responsibility for any loss or damage incurred as a result of this book.

British Library Cataloguing in Publication Data
A catalogue record for this book is available from the British Library.

Produced by Hart McLeod, Cambridge
Commissioned by Helen Clark
Project management by Julia Swales
Editing by Pat Winter
Cover design by Bigtop Design, Bicester
Internal design by Bigtop Design, Bicester
Illustrations by Ken Vail Graphic Design and Jeff Edwards
Production by PDQ
Printed and bound in Italy

Contents

Linnaeus and the classification system	2	Extinctions	59
Superorganism	7	Fish farming	65
Forensic entomologists	14	GM crops	69
Sharks – the profile of a predator	19	Pesticides versus biological control	72
Behaviour of wild animals	28	Global warming and flooding	76
Responding to the seasons	37	The need for sustainable development	81
Animal adaptations	43	Life on Mars	88
Peppered moths	49	Answers	92
Lichens and air pollution	54	Index and glossary	97

How to use this book

Key Ideas: Interdependence can be used as enrichment material to motivate and enthuse students following any KS3 science course. The 16 chapters of stimulating, cross-curricular scientific accounts and activities provide up-to-the-minute information on subjects such as over-fishing and its impact on food chains, how insects are used to help solve crime, and GM crops – for and against. They also cover subjects of general topical and historical interest, such as sharks as top predators, and the dark peppered moth as evidence of natural selection.

Each chapter consists of: an introduction; texts and activities; a review; and a unit summary. The activities cover a range of learning styles and can be used as class or group assignments, or enrichment exercises for individual pupils. To help you select material for lessons covering particular topics and skills, the grid on pages iv and v links Framework objectives with the relevant chapters. In the grid:

- I = Interdependence
- SE = Scientific Enquiry Sc1
- Objectives are numbered consecutively, following the same order as the Framework for Teaching Science.

Answers to the activities that are closed appear on pages 92–96, and key words in the text are defined in an index and glossary on pages 97–99.

Key to coloured panels in the chapters

- lab experiments and web search activities
- written and group discussion activities
- research, evidence and scientific developments boxes
- interesting facts boxes

Key to symbols in activities boxes

- lab activity
- hazards that may be encountered during an experiment
- literacy activity
- web search activity
- numeracy activity
- ICT activity, e.g. PowerPoint
- Sc1 practice activity

Framework objectives matched to material in this book

Teaching objective	Related chapters
Y7 I1	Linnaeus and the classification system, 2 Superorganism, 7 Forensic entomologists, 14 Sharks – the profile of a predator, 19 Behaviour of wild animals, 28
Y7 I2	Sharks – the profile of a predator, 19
Y7 I3	Sharks – the profile of a predator, 19 Behaviour of wild animals, 28 Responding to the seasons, 37 Animal adaptations, 43 Peppered moths, 49 Extinctions, 59
Y7 SE1	Superorganism, 7 Forensic entomologists, 14 Behaviour of wild animals, 28 Peppered moths, 49
Y7 SE2	Responding to the seasons, 37 Lichens and air pollution, 54 Pesticides versus biological control, 72
Y7 SE3	Behaviour of wild animals, 28 Responding to the seasons, 37 Pesticides versus biological control, 72 Global warming and flooding, 76
Y7 SE4	Forensic entomologists, 14 Sharks – the profile of a predator, 19 Behaviour of wild animals, 28 Responding to the seasons, 37 Peppered moths, 49 Global warming and flooding, 76

Teaching objective	Related chapters
Y7 SE5	Behaviour of wild animals 28 Animal adaptations, 43 Peppered moths, 49
Y7 SE6	Forensic entomologists, 14 Sharks – the profile of a predator, 19 Behaviour of wild animals, 28 Responding to the seasons, 37 Lichens and air pollution, 54 Global warming and flooding, 76
Y7 SE7	Sharks – the profile of a predator, 19 Behaviour of wild animals, 28 Responding to the seasons, 37 Peppered moths, 49 Lichens and air pollution, 54 Global warming and flooding, 76
Y7 SE8	Behaviour of wild animals, 28 Lichens and air pollution, 54
Y8 I1	Linnaeus and the classification system, 2
Y8 I2	Forensic entomologists, 14 Sharks – the profile of a predator, 19 Fish farming, 65
Y8 SE2	Behaviour of wild animals, 28 Peppered moths, 49
Y8 SE3	Forensic entomologists, 14 Peppered moths, 49 Extinctions, 59 Life on Mars, 88

Teaching objective	Related chapters
Y8 SE4	Forensic entomologists, 14 Sharks – the profile of a predator, 19 Behaviour of wild animals, 28 Responding to the seasons, 37 Animal adaptations, 43 Peppered moths, 49 Global warming and flooding, 76 The need for sustainable development, 81
Y8 SE5	Behaviour of wild animals, 28 Responding to the seasons, 37 Peppered moths, 49 Lichens and air pollution, 54 Pesticides versus biological control, 72
Y8 SE6	Sharks – the profile of a predator, 19 Behaviour of wild animals, 28 Responding to the seasons, 37 Peppered moths, 49 Lichens and air pollution, 54
Y8 SE7	Behaviour of wild animals, 28 Lichens and air pollution, 54
Y9 I1	Fish farming, 65 GM crops, 69 Pesticides versus biological control, 72 The need for sustainable development, 81
Y9 I2	Responding to the seasons, 37 Peppered moths, 49 Lichens and air pollution, 54 Extinctions, 59 Global warming and flooding, 76 The need for sustainable development, 81 Life on Mars, 88

Teaching objective	Related chapters
Y9 I3	Forensic entomologists, 14 Responding to the seasons, 37 The need for sustainable development, 81
Y9 SE1	Linnaeus and the classification system, 2 Forensic entomologists, 14 Peppered moths, 49 Fish farming, 65 GM crops, 69 Pesticides versus biological control, 72 Global warming and flooding, 76 The need for sustainable development, 81 Life on Mars, 88
Y9 SE2	Responding to the seasons, 37
Y9 SE4	Behaviour of wild animals, 28
Y9 SE5	Behaviour of wild animals, 28 Responding to the seasons, 37
Y9 SE6	Behaviour of wild animals, 28 Peppered moths, 49 Lichens and air pollution, 54 Global warming and flooding, 76
Y9 SE7	Behaviour of wild animals, 28

Linnaeus and the classification system

Introduction

In this chapter, we learn about the classification of organisms into groups and the system developed by Linnaeus.

- Organisms are living things.
- Living things are classified into groups based on their similarities.
- A group of organisms that are so similar to each other that they can reproduce together are classified as a species.

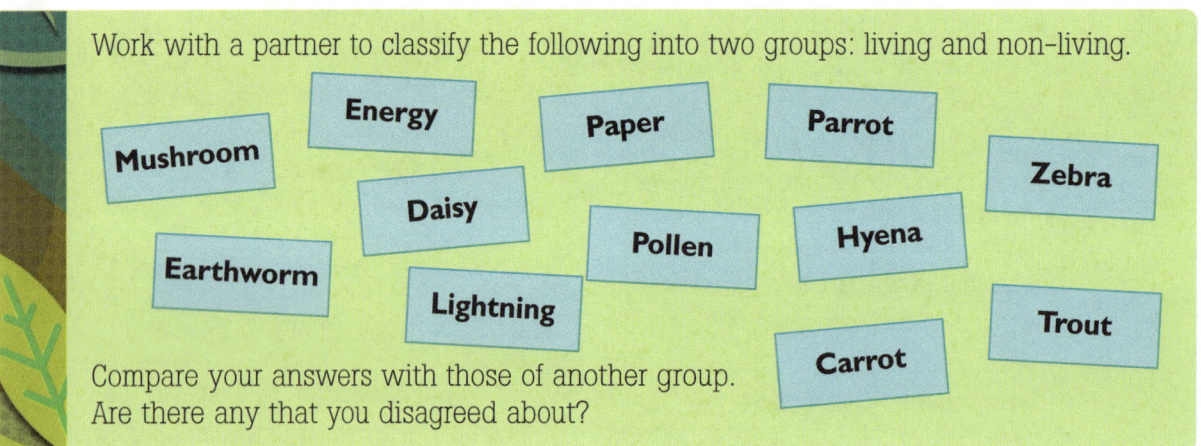

Work with a partner to classify the following into two groups: living and non-living.

Mushroom, Energy, Paper, Parrot, Zebra, Daisy, Pollen, Hyena, Earthworm, Lightning, Carrot, Trout

Compare your answers with those of another group. Are there any that you disagreed about?

Classification

All classification, whether in science or anywhere else, is just a system of organising information, to make it easier for us to recognise and describe things. Scientists use seven characteristics to decide whether things are living or non-living. These characteristics can be remembered using MRS GREN:

However, there is a problem with this way of classifying, because not all the characteristics apply to viruses. Viruses do not really respire and they can remain inactive for very long periods of time. So, are they living organisms? Some scientists believe they are, but this would mean redefining the characteristics of living things to include viruses. For the time being, the question is unresolved.

- **M** = Movement; all living things can move
- **R** = Respiration; all living things respire to release energy from their food
- **S** = Sensitivity; all living things can sense stimuli in their environment
- **G** = Growth; all living things grow bigger
- **R** = Reproduction; all living things reproduce
- **E** = Excretion; all living things excrete waste from their body
- **N** = Nutrition; all living things need food to give them energy

In biology, all organisms are further classified by being put in groups with similar characteristics, such as genetic relationships and physical features. The study of the classification of organisms is called taxonomy – plants and animals are put into taxonomic groups based on their similarities. Scientists learn and understand more all the time about the organisms that survive on this planet and so taxonomic groups are constantly being reviewed and altered.

> **1** On your own, classify the following into groups, with reasons to explain why you have put them together.
>
> | Crab | Snail | Penguin |
> |---|---|---|
> | Whale | Rabbit | Shark |
> | Sparrow | Horse | Snake |
> | Frog | Bat | Goldfish |
> | Spider | Fly | Ostrich |
> | Worm | Turtle | Moth |
>
> **2** Swap your classification system with a partner. Check to see whether any of the animals could actually be placed in more than one group.

Artificial and natural classification

If we classified all animals that can fly into one group, then birds, bats and insects would all be together. This is an artificial group because it is based on only one characteristic that the animals have in common. Birds, bats and insects are actually very different types of animals.

Another example of an artificial group would be to put all yellow flowers together. This would mean that dandelions, daffodils and yellow roses would all be classified in the same group.

Biologists use a natural classification system, which is based on evolution. Organisms are grouped together because in evolutionary terms they are related. This means that they have evolved over many years from the same ancestors. The more recent their common ancestors are, the more characteristics they will have in common, because the genetic information inside the nucleus of their cells will be very similar.

> **3** Find out the meanings of the following words.
> evolution
> ancestor
> genes
> nucleus
>
> **4** Copy and complete the following table to show how many characteristics the listed animals have in common, and how many characteristics are different.
>
> | Animals | Similarities | Differences |
> |---|---|---|
> | Birds, bats and insects | | |
>
> **5** Copy and complete the following table to show how many characteristics these plants have in common and how many characteristics are different.
>
> | Plants | Similarities | Differences |
> |---|---|---|
> | Dandelions, daffodils and roses | | |

The development of the classification system

Even before people understood the theory of evolution, they realised how useful it would be to classify organisms into groups based on their similarities.

Aristotle developed the first known classification system in 384 BC. Linnaeus then worked out the system which, with modifications, we still use today, and he explained it in his book *Systema Naturae* in 1735.

- **Kingdom** e.g. Animals: organisms that eat other organisms
- **Phylum** e.g. Vertebrates: animals with a backbone
- **Class** e.g. Mammals: vertebrates that feed their young on milk
- **Order** e.g. Primates: mammals with large brains, and five fingers and toes
- **Family** e.g. Hominids: primates that look similar to man
- **Genus** e.g. *Homo*: hominids that walk upright
- **Species** e.g. *sapiens*: humans

Aristotle introduced the word 'genus' to describe a group of similar organisms, but the names of individual organisms were constantly changing because different people called them different things.

Carl Linnaeus, who was born in Sweden in 1707, studied for a medical degree and then practised medicine and lectured medical students. His hobby, however, was botany – the study of plants. He worked painstakingly and with brilliance to produce *Systema Naturae* and added to it over the years. Its 10th edition published in 1758 and his book *Species Plantarum*, published in 1753, remain the starting point for the naming (nomenclature) of plants and animals today.

In Linnaeus's nomenclature, he grouped organisms using what is known as the binomial system – each organism is given two names in Latin, the genus name and the species name. This means that people all around the world can then name and talk about an organism, knowing that they actually mean the same organism.

A species is a group of organisms that have many characteristics in common. This similarity makes it possible for them to mate with each other and produce young that are also able to mate and have young of their own.

Organisms of the same species have more in common with each other than organisms in the same kingdom, or any other group above 'species' in the flow chart. As you move down through the classification system, the organisms in the same group have more and more characteristics in common.

Linnaeus became known as the father of taxonomy. An international society for the study of nature was set up in London a few years after he died and was named after him. The Linnaean Society of London continues to thrive today.

In his own time, many students whom Linnaeus taught helped him to update his books by sending him plants from all over the world whenever they visited a new country. His most famous student was Daniel Solander who travelled with Captain Cook on his first voyage around the world.

Since then, the binomial system has continued to develop as scientists have added more groups in between those Linnaeus created. Taxonomy continues to be studied today, and in 1995 the International Committee on Bionomenclature reviewed the naming of all organisms, and decided that the system in place was still useful for modern scientists.

Latin names overcome language barriers

The following extract describes how useful Latin names of animals can be. It is taken from David Attenborough's memoirs. It is the 1950s and he has just met a local guide, called Sabran, who is to help him find Komodo dragons in the wild.

> Talking to him was not easy for I still had not acquired much conversational Indonesian, but he and I soon evolved a pidgin of our own which served our particular requirements. One morning as we were steaming slowly up-river, he called me and pointed excitedly to a tree on the bank.
>
> 'Barung ada,' he said. That I understood. There had been a bird there. 'Apa?' I said, meaning – what kind of bird?
>
> His answer to that, however, defeated me. He repeated it several times but I was baffled.
>
> Then he said 'Irena puella.' And that I understood immediately. It had been a fairy bluebird. Sabran knew the scientific name from his time as a zoo collector and I from my study of the field guide to the birds of South-east Asia. I was delighted by the thought that he, who had never left his native Borneo, and I, a stranger from England, should have been able to make ourselves mutually understood by speaking the dog-Latin that European scholars had used during the eighteenth century.
>
> David Attenborough, *Life on Air*, BBC Books 2003

6 Find out the common names of these mammals.

Bison bison
Pan troglodytes
Felis lynx
Panthera tigris
Orcinus orca
Canis lupis

7 Calculate the number of years between Aristotle's work on classification and the work of Linnaeus.

8 Visit these websites to find out more about Linnaeus.
www.nhm.ac.uk/library/linn
www.linnean.org/contents/history/linnaeus_biography.html

Review

Work with a partner to copy and complete this table.

Vertebrate group	Characteristics of the group
Fish	
Amphibians	
Reptiles	
Birds	
Mammals	

Chapter summary

In this chapter you have found out that:
- There are 7 characteristics of life.
- Classification is a system used by people to organise organisms into groups.
- Taxonomy is the study of classification.
- Organisms of the same species have more characteristics in common than organisms of different species.

Superorganism

Introduction

In this chapter, we look at how a group of organisms belonging to the same species work together to increase their chances of survival.

- In the classification system, organisms are grouped together because of their similarities.
- A species is a collection of organisms grouped together because they are so similar that they can reproduce with each other.
- A superorganism is a group of individuals of the same species living together in a colony.

Look at the following classification system.

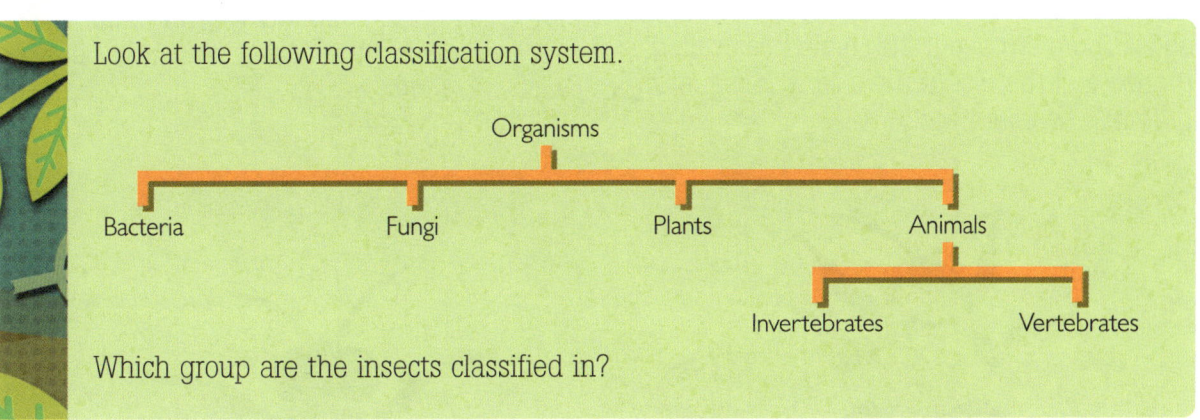

Which group are the insects classified in?

Social insects

There are some species of insect that live together in a group. The group is known as a colony. Since they all have the same mother, each individual insect in the colony is related to all the other insects because they are all brothers and sisters. There is division of labour within the colony, with every member carrying out a different job to keep the whole colony alive – they need each other to survive, which is why together they are often called a superorganism.

Social insects are superorganisms and they include species of bees, termites, ants and wasps.

The Western honeybee, *Apis mellifera*, is a perfect example of a social insect. Honeybees are useful to humans because they pollinate flowers and they produce honey which we can eat.

> 1 Draw a series of labelled diagrams to show how bees cross-pollinate flowers. Include the anthers and stigma of the flowers.

A honeybee colony

Honeybees live in hives, either that humans build or that they build themselves. The bees use a landing stage to get in and out of the hive. Inside the hive are thousands of little boxes, called cells, that are made of wax. If beekeepers have not provided the cells, the bees make them. Many of the cells are in the brood area – the section of the hive where eggs are laid. This is in the centre of the hive, where it is warmest. The other cells have food stored inside them and are sealed with wax when they are full.

The colony inside a hive may contain 50 000 bees. One of these bees is the queen – the only female in the whole colony that can lay eggs. There are about 250 male bees called drones and the rest of the colony is made up of female worker bees.

Eggs that can develop into queen bees are laid in the largest brood cells. When they hatch, the larvae are fed a very rich food, called royal jelly, for 5 days. They then pupate into adult queen bees bigger than every other type of bee. There can only be one queen in a hive. The section on Swarming (page 12) explains what happens next.

> **2** Look at the diagrams of the queen bee and the drone. List the differences in their body structure and try to explain why you think this is.
>
> **3** Using the information given here, calculate the number of worker bees in a colony.

A queen honeybee. *A drone.*

The body of the worker honeybee

Each of the **front legs** has a row of hairs called a **pollen comb** that is used to comb the pollen off the body of the bee. There is also a second row of hairs that the bees use to clean their eyes.

The **middle legs** have tiny spikes to scoop **wax** out of the glands in the abdomen and to unload the pollen baskets.

The **intestine** has a section called the **nectar sac** where nectar is stored until the bee gets back to the hive.

A worker bee.

- head
- thorax
- abdomen (with wax glands and intestines inside)
- front leg with pollen combs
- middle leg with spikes
- wings (2 pairs)
- back leg
- stings

The **back legs** carry the pollen while the bee flies from flowers back to the hive. The pollen is squashed around the legs and stuck together with a little nectar. It forms what are called **pollen baskets**.

The **mandibles** are like teeth that can chew pollen and wax, and can also be used to bite any attacking insects.

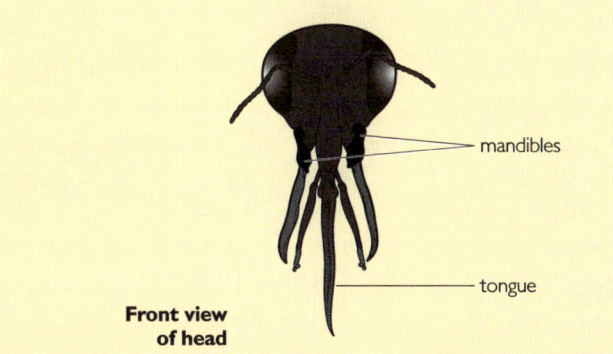

- mandibles
- tongue

Front view of head

The **tongue** of the worker bee is folded up when not in use, but is a long tube that can suck up nectar from inside flowers.

At the very end of the abdomen is a **sac of venom** with two **stings** that can be used during an attack.

4 Copy and complete the following table using information from the text.

Structures of the worker bee body	How each is adapted to carry out its functions

The life of the worker bee

Worker bees live as adults for about 40 days. Throughout their life, they carry out numerous jobs for the benefit of the whole colony.

Days	Stages in the life of a worker bee and the jobs they carry out
0	Fertilised eggs are laid by the queen in small cells in the brood area.
3	Each egg hatches and a larva without any legs wriggles out.
3–5	The larvae are fed with royal jelly.
6–7	The larvae are now fed watery nectar and pollen. This change in diet stops them developing into queen bees. During this time the larvae grow and shed their skin a number of times.
8–14	The larvae are sealed in their cells with wax while they pupate into adult worker bees.
14	Each adult bee bites through the wax and comes out of its cell.
14–20	The young adults clean the cells by removing skins that the larvae have shed and any dead bees. The rubbish is taken to the landing stage and dropped out of the hive. This cleaning reduces the spread of infection. The queen can then lay more eggs in the empty cells.
21–27	The workers now develop a gland in the mouth known as the nurse gland. This gland makes the royal jelly, which is fed to larvae. They seem to know how much royal jelly to give to each larva to control whether it will develop into a worker bee or a queen.
28–31	The bees stop producing royal jelly at this point and start making wax instead. This means that they can work on building new cells and repairing the hive. The cells vary in size but are about 2.5 cm deep, sloping backwards back-to-back with each other. The wax is chewed until it is soft enough to mould into shape. During this time, the worker bees also start to take their first flights out of the hive to learn their way around.
32–34	The workers change jobs again, becoming guards. They stand on the landing stage checking every bee that arrives to make sure it belongs to their colony. They recognise their own by the scent. It is important that the bees guard their hive because other bees and wasps may try to enter to steal the honey they have stored inside. Any robbers that arrive are driven away or even stung to death.
35–55	For the rest of their life, the workers go out of the hive every day to collect nectar and pollen from flowers. The nectar is eaten but is stored in a sac in the intestine. During its flight, a bee keeps pumping the nectar into its mouth and then swallowing it again. This makes the nectar more concentrated because water is lost by evaporation. Enzymes are also added to it, which begin to change the nectar into honey. The pollen is held in the pollen baskets on the back legs. When the bee returns to the hive, the pollen is taken away by younger adult worker bees so it can be stored in cells. The nectar is regurgitated and passed into the mouths of other bees that take it to a cell where it will stay until the enzymes have completed the change of nectar into honey. It takes the nectar from approximately 8000 flowers to make just 1 gram of honey. The pollen and honey are sealed inside cells with wax. During the winter when there is very little food outside, the bees will go to their food stores to use up what they collected during the summer months.

5 What does pupate mean? Can you name another insect that pupates?

6 Choose from the following the organisms that spread infections.
  a bacteria
  b fungi
  c viruses
  d all of these

7 Nectar is a sugary liquid. Investigate the effect of evaporation on the concentration of a sugar solution.

This is what you need:
- 50 cm³ of water in a 75 cm³ beaker
- balance
- 1 g sugar, measured
- glass stirring rod
- Bunsen burner, heatproof mat, tripod, gauze
- evaporating basin

This is what you do:

1 Add the sugar to the water and stir until it dissolves

> ⚠ Wear safety spectacles during this experiment, and take care with hot equipment.

2 Pour a small amount into an evaporating basin

3 Heat the basin over a half-blue Bunsen flame

4 As the water evaporates, keep adding more of the sugar solution until the beaker is empty

5 Describe what you can see in the evaporating basin when all the water has evaporated

8 What is an enzyme?

9 Calculate how many flowers the bees need to collect nectar from to make 25 g of honey.

In his play 'King Henry the Fifth' Act 1, Scene 2, Shakespeare compares the lives of a bee colony to the lives of people. Notice that he says the bees have a king instead of a queen. Did he not know that the bee controlling the hive is a female, or did he do this on purpose?

> Therefore doth heaven divide
> The state of man in divers functions,
> Setting endeavour in continual motion;
> To which is fixed as an aim or butt
> Obedience; for so work the honey bees,
> Creatures that by a rule in nature teach
> The act of order to a peopled kingdom.
> They have a king, and officers of sorts,
> Where some like magistrates correct at home;
> Others like merchants venture trade abroad;
> Others like soldiers, armed in their stings,
> Make boot upon the summer's velvet buds,
> Which pillage they with merry march bring home
> To the tent-royal of their emperor;
> Who, busied in his majesty, surveys
> The singing masons building roofs of gold,
> The civil citizens kneading up the honey,
> The poor mechanic porters crowding in
> Their heavy burdens at his narrow gate,
> The sad-ey'd justice, with his surly hum,
> Delivering o'er to executors pale
> The lazy yawning drone.

Communication

A superorganism contains thousands of individuals, so it is important for them all to be able to communicate with each other. They recognise members of their colony using the antennae to touch and smell each other.

Workers that have been out foraging for pollen and nectar communicate where they have found the food when they get back into the hive. They do this by performing the wiggle dance that is explained by the Austrian scientist Karl von Frisch in his book *The Dancing Bees*.

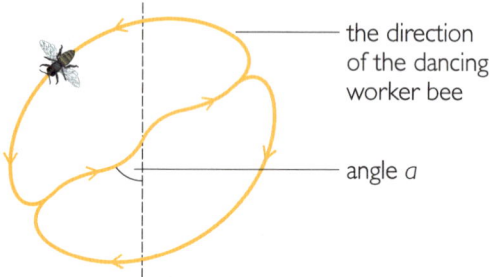

Dance of the worker bee.

The bee moves around in a figure-of-eight. If the middle section of the dance is directed upwards, it means that the food is straight towards the Sun. If downwards, it means that the food is away from the Sun. The angle *a* of the middle section of the dance is the same as the angle between the food and the Sun.

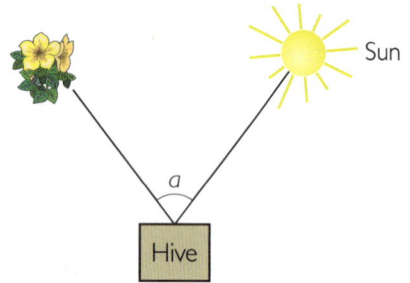

So, amazingly, bees are able to calculate the position of the food relative to the Sun, even though it moves across the sky during the day. When the Sun is covered by cloud, they can just use the difference in the light levels of the sky to identify its position.

During the middle section of the dance the bee wiggles its abdomen. The length of this section represents the distance the food is from the hive, so the closer the food, the faster the bee will move through its wiggle dance.

Every so often, the bee stops dancing to regurgitate food. The other bees taste it so they can decide how good the food is and will be able to recognise it when they find it.

Sometimes, the hive is too dark for the workers to actually see the dancing bee, but they can still understand the information by picking up the vibrations of the dance.

> **10** List the different types of information that the dancing bee gives to other bees about a food source.

Worker bees are constantly looking after the queen bee by feeding and cleaning her. As they do this, they pick up a chemical from her body known as 'queen substance'. Whenever the workers come into contact with each other, the queen substance is passed between them and this signals to all the bees in the hive that the queen is present.

Swarming

There comes a time when the queen leaves the hive, with approximately half of her workers, to go and start a new colony somewhere else. Thousands of bees fly out of the hive together in a swarm. They usually land on a nearby tree waiting for scout bees to find a suitable place to build a new hive.

Swarming happens when the colony starts to get too big for the hive. There isn't enough queen substance to spread around when there are so many bees in the colony. This triggers some of the workers to start rearing new queens. They feed royal jelly to some of the larvae for the full five days. The first queen bees to pupate destroy all the others and then fight each other to the death until only one remains. In this way, the remaining new queen will be the strongest and the fittest.

The young queen flies from the hive followed by drones. She will mate with a number of drones, who might be from her own hive or from a different colony. She stores the sperm in her abdomen and will use it to fertilise her eggs for the rest of her life, which is usually two years but could be as many as five.

She returns to the original hive and starts laying eggs. The old queen leaves in a swarm to set up a new colony somewhere else.

 Web Links

Visit these websites to find out more about honeybee superorganisms:

www.honey.com/kids/facts.html
www.insecta-inspecta.com/bees/honey/ index
www.pbs.org/wgbh/nova/bees/
www.csl.gov.uk/science/organ/environ/bee/ index.cfm

 ## Review

Write your own poem describing the life of a honeybee colony. Include information from this chapter to help you explain life inside the hive.

 ## Chapter summary

In this chapter you have found out that:
- Some species of insect survive by living together in a colony.
- There is division of labour within a honeybee colony.
- The bees have to communicate with each other to function as a superorganism.

Forensic entomologists

Introduction

In this chapter, we look at the work of forensic entomologists.

- Identification of organisms to species level can be put to good use.
- Decomposers are organisms that feed off dead and decaying matter.
- Decomposers recycle the materials in an environment.
- The work of scientists can help the police to solve crimes.

Get thinking with a partner: Can you solve this mystery? Picture an old barn in a field by a river. A body is found locked in the cellar. It is discovered that the person died by drowning but the body was not moved after death. How is this possible?

What is forensic entomology?

Entomology is the study of insects. Insects are invertebrate animals that have six legs, three parts to the body, and usually a pair of wings. Scientists know of about $1\frac{1}{2}$ million different species of insect around the world. They can be very difficult to identify because of their size. What makes it even more difficult is that there could be another 10 million species of insect that have yet to be discovered and classified.

Entomologists are scientists who specialise in the study of insects. They might even concentrate on just one particular species, as there is still a lot to learn about practically all of them.

Forensic entomologists use their knowledge of insects to help the police solve crimes. When a human or any other organism dies, the body immediately becomes a source of food for the decomposers. Decomposers are organisms that break down dead tissue as they feed on it. Bacteria, fungi, worms and many species of insect are decomposers.

By examining the insects feeding on a dead body, the forensic entomologists can estimate the time of death, and can even work out whether the body has been moved after death.

1 What is an invertebrate animal?

2 Use this key to identify the insects pictured.

1. Insect has yellow and black stripes = **wasp**
   If not, go to 2

2. Insect has wings, go to 3
   Insect does not have wings, go to 4

3. Wings are covered in hard outer cases = **beetle**
   Wings not covered = **blowfly**

4. Insect has large head and broad waist = **termite**
   Insect has a narrow waist = **ant**

The decomposers

Decomposers are important organisms in the environment because they recycle the minerals in it.

Plants use minerals from the soil as they grow, so the minerals get built into the plants. Herbivores obtain these minerals when they eat plants. Carnivores get their minerals when they eat the herbivores. In this way, the minerals are passed along the food chain. When the plants and animals die, the decomposers eat their bodies and break them down. Their waste then returns the minerals to the soil. Plants can then use these minerals in the soil to help them grow and so the cycle begins all over again.

The first decomposers to begin feeding and growing on a dead body are the bacteria. As they reproduce and start multiplying, the bacteria give off a smell.

Insects called blue-bottles and green-bottles (also known as blowflies) can smell this from nearly 3000 m away. They fly towards the source of the smell because here they know they will find food and a suitable place to lay their eggs.

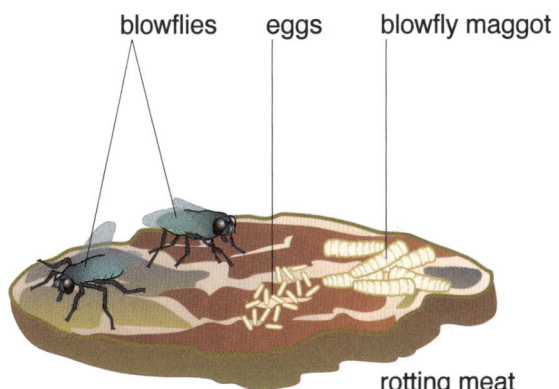

After just a few hours (although it does depend on the physical conditions of the environment) a dead body can be covered with thousands of eggs. A maggot hatches out of each egg and wriggles deep into the body, feeding as it goes.

15

As it grows, it sheds its skin. The weather affects how quickly maggots grow – warmer temperatures speed up their development. Eventually, the maggots pupate into adult flies.

Different species of insects pass through this life cycle at different rates.

After a time, which is again dependent on the weather, all that will be left of the body is a pile of bones.

3 a What is a herbivore?

b What is a carnivore?

c What is an omnivore?

4 Bacteria reproduce by dividing into two. If a bacterium reproduces every 30 minutes, how many bacteria will there be after 5 hours?

5 Put these stages in the life cycle of a blowfly into the correct order:

| Pupa | Egg | Fly | Maggot |

The start of forensic entomology

Date	Country	What happened
13th century	China	A man was stabbed. The knives of all the local people were laid out. One of them was attracting blowflies. This was because it had blood smeared on it, even though it had been wiped to look clean. The owner broke down and confessed to the murder.
1855	France	The body of a baby was found in a house. The decay that had been caused by insects feeding on the body suggested that the baby had been dead for a number of years. This meant that the new owners of the house could not have been responsible, and a hunt began for the previous people who had lived there.
1935	Britain	Two women were found dead. Dr Mearns, an entomologist, was asked by the police to examine the maggots growing in the bodies. His evidence helped the police to conclude that the killer had been the husband of one of the women; the other woman was her maid. Dr Mearns became the first forensic entomologist in the country. The husband was hanged for his crimes.
1947	Netherlands	For the first time, a forensic entomologist, called Professor Leclercq, gave evidence in court.

6 a Use an atlas of the world to find the position of China, France, Britain and the Netherlands.

b Visit these websites to find out more about forensic entomology:

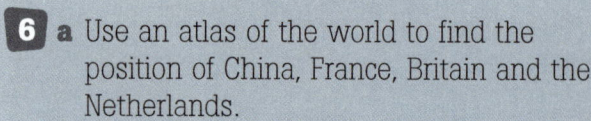

www.forensic-entomology.com/
www.missouri.edu/~agwww/entomology/
www.key-net.net/users/swb/forensics/

Dr. Bug and the blowfly body

Dr. Bug is a specialist in the life cycle of the blowfly.

1. Dr. Bug, I'm afraid we need your help. We've found a body and we think it might be a murder case.

2. At the crime scene

3. I need to know about the temperature and the weather conditions to help me work out how quickly the maggots have grown.

4. The courts will need the evidence I collect.

5. We're going to let these maggots finish their life cycle. Adult flies are easier to identify than maggots.

6. Now I know the species and the weather conditions, I'll be able to estimate the time of death.

7. Thank you Dr. Bug, that might just be the evidence we need to convict the murderer.

7 Discuss with a partner why you think Dr Bug is wearing protective clothes at the crime scene. Compare your answers with another group before feeding back to the rest of the class.

8   Use a temperature probe and data logger to take recordings of the temperature of the air over 24 hours. Print out a graph of the results. Mark on the graph when you think maggots might grow fastest.

Review

Draw a food chain that shows a producer, a primary consumer, a secondary consumer and decomposers. Position the arrows to show the direction of the energy flow.

Chapter summary

In this chapter you have found out that:
- Forensic entomologists use their knowledge of insect life cycles to help solve crimes.
- Keys are used to help identify different species of organisms.
- Decomposers recycle the minerals in the environment by feeding on dead organisms.

Sharks – the profile of a predator

Introduction

In this chapter, we look at the shark as an example of a predator.

- Sharks belong to the vertebrate group of fish.
- Sharks are adapted to live in water.
- Sharks are extremely successful predators.

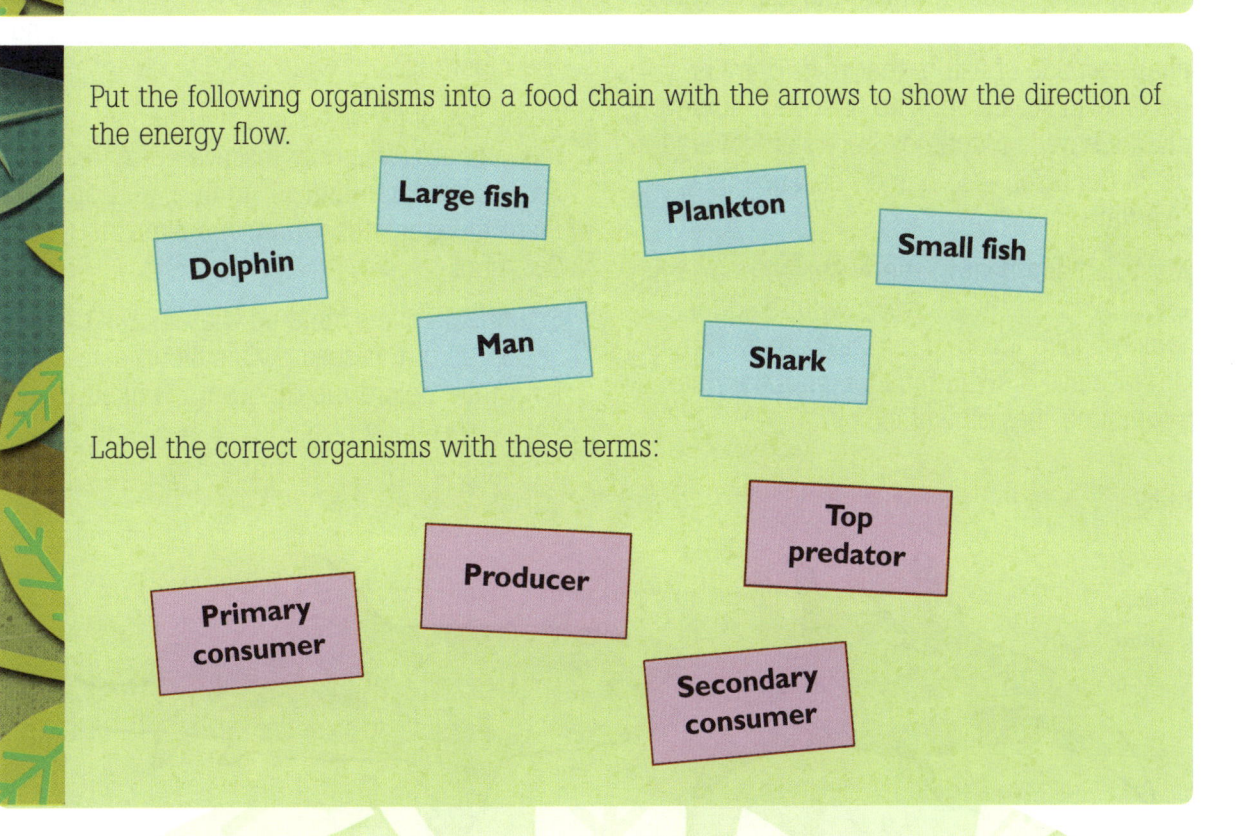

Put the following organisms into a food chain with the arrows to show the direction of the energy flow.

- Large fish
- Dolphin
- Plankton
- Small fish
- Man
- Shark

Label the correct organisms with these terms:

- Producer
- Top predator
- Primary consumer
- Secondary consumer

Classification of sharks

Sharks are classified as vertebrates. They are grouped together with other fish but they have a skeleton of cartilage instead of bone. Cartilage is softer than bone and is like the gristle we have in our ears and at the end of our nose. This makes the shark's body very flexible so that it can twist and move very easily in the water.

Other fish with cartilage skeletons are the skates and rays, so they are all put together in a fish group called the Elasmobranchs.

All fish have gills for breathing, but the Elasmobranchs do not have the flap covering the gill slits that other fish have. Another characteristic of fish is that their body is covered in scales. Instead of scales, however, sharks have a tough, leathery skin covered in small denticles – so named because they look like flat teeth.

Most fish can float in the water without any effort because they have a swim bladder, which is like a bag of air inside them. Sharks do not have a swim bladder, so if they stop swimming they slowly sink.

Generally, fish lay eggs, but most sharks actually give birth to live young. The great white shark has a litter of between 2 and 14 babies that are over a metre long when they are born. Some sharks do lay eggs, and each egg is inside a protective case known as a mermaid's purse that is attached to seaweed or a rock. Once born, all baby sharks have to fend for themselves, as there is no parental care.

There are about 350 species of shark in the world. Over half of them are less than 1 m long, but the biggest, the whale sharks, can grow to 19 m. Whale sharks are as long as a tennis court and as heavy as a truck. The tail fin is 4 m high, their skin is 20 cm thick, and the mouth is 1 m wide.

A species of shark, which was named megamouth, was only discovered in 1976. Sharks are quite difficult to find, and only 13 more megamouths were seen over the next 23 years.

Scientists have estimated that sharks first appeared in our seas 400 million years ago, a long time before the dinosaurs walked the Earth. The body of the shark has hardly changed between then and now.

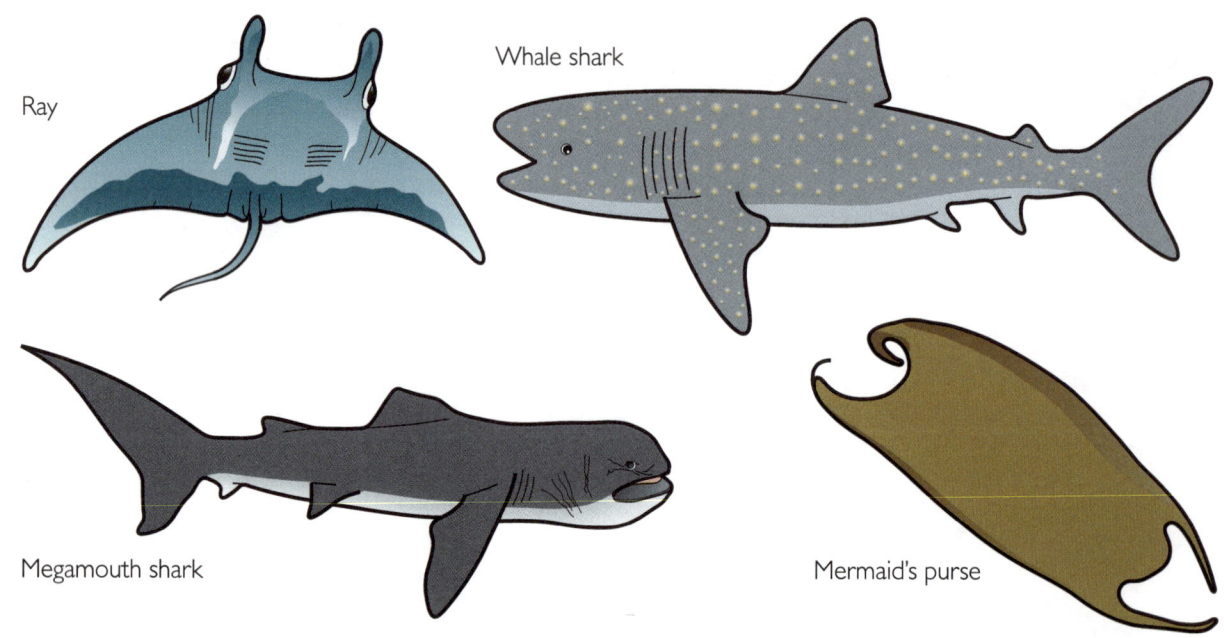

Ray

Whale shark

Megamouth shark

Mermaid's purse

1 Make a table with two columns. In the first column list all the similarities between sharks and other fish, and in the second column list the differences.

2 Visit this website to find out about life in the seas millions of years ago:
bbc.co.uk/sn
and click on Sea Monsters.

The habitat of sharks

Most species of shark live in the sea and are adapted to the salt water, but some live in lakes and rivers. They prefer warm tropical waters like the Indian Ocean, but they have been found as far north as Britain and as far south as Antarctica. The waters off the coast of KwaZulu-Natal in South Africa have more sharks swimming in them than anywhere else in the world.

Different species of shark inhabit different depths of water. Most prefer to be near the surface where it is warmer and they are closer to their prey. Others, for example megamouth, swim deep in the open ocean, which is why we very rarely see them. Wobbegongs, however, live on the seabed close to the shore.

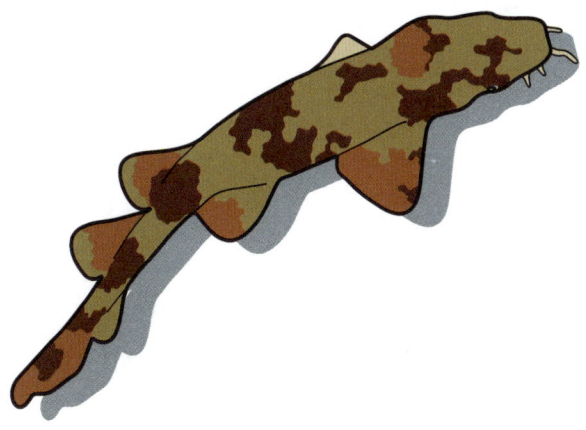

Wobbegong shark.

Scientists can tag sharks with radio transmitters. The transmitter sends a signal up to a satellite that is out in space orbiting the Earth. The satellite bounces the signal back down to Earth so that scientists can track the movements of their shark. Using this method, it has been found that great white sharks can travel over 300 miles a day but normally swim at an average speed of just 2 miles an hour. The transmitter provides the scientist with information for a few months until the battery runs out.

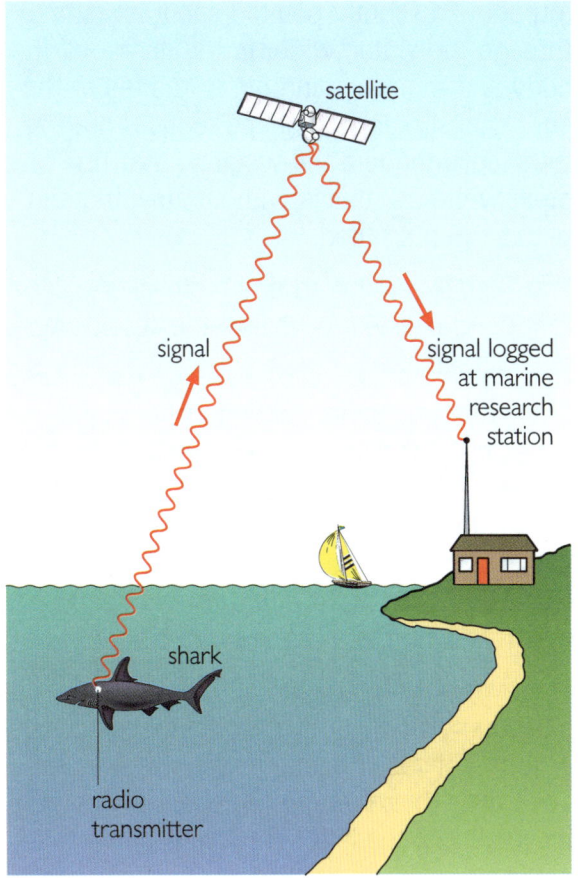

3 You will need a photocopy of a map of the world and an atlas. Mark on the following places:

Indian Ocean, Britain, Antarctica, and South Africa.

4 Calculate how many miles the great white shark can swim in 48 hours.

Adaptations to life in the water

The design of the body of sharks makes them fantastic swimmers. They propel themselves through the water by moving their tail from side to side. They use two sets of fins on the side, called the pectoral fins, for steering and braking. The fin on their back that sticks out of the water when they swim near the surface is called the dorsal fin.

Great whites have a body shaped like a torpedo – a slightly pointed snout for cutting through the water, wider in the middle of the body and then thinning out to the tail at the end. This streamlined shape reduces drag as they move through the water so that the great white can cruise without stopping and without getting tired.

The skin, covered with tiny tooth-like scales that point backwards, makes the shark even more streamlined.

Sharks have to swim continuously to make water move through their gills and allow oxygen to be absorbed from it. If sharks stop swimming, they can drown! The liver of a shark contains large amounts of fat, which is less dense than water and helps to keep them afloat without the aid of a swim bladder.

The eyes are on the side of the head for good all-round vision, but sharks cannot see colours or form a detailed image in the way we can. Their eyes, however, are excellent at spotting movement at the low light levels found under water.

Catching and eating prey

All sharks are solitary hunters and although they may be found together in a group, each animal is out for itself and will even attack and feed on other sharks.

The biggest sharks are not actually hunters. Whale sharks and basking sharks filter-feed

5 Investigate the effect of streamlining on speed.

You will need:
- 100 cm³ measuring cylinder
- a thick liquid, e.g. glycerol
- plasticine
- thread
- balance
- light gates connected to a data logger

This is what you do:

1. Pour 100 cm³ of the liquid into the measuring cylinder
2. Set up the light gates, one around the top of the measuring cylinder at the liquid's surface and one at the base
3. Set up the data logger to measure speed from between light gate 1 and light gate 2
4. Measure the mass of a piece of plasticine
5. Shape the plasticine and attach a long piece of thread to it so that you can pull it back out of the measuring cylinder
6. Lower the shape into the cylinder and collect a measurement of its speed as it sinks through the liquid
7. Repeat with a number of different shapes, making sure that each is made from the same mass of plasticine
8. Interpret the results. Was the most streamlined shape the fastest?

6 Sharks have large amounts of fat in the liver to help them stay afloat. This is because the oil is less dense than water. Observe that oil can float on water and explain their difference in density using the idea of particles.

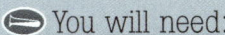 You will need:
- measuring cylinder of water
- oil

This is what you do:

1. Pour oil into the measuring cylinder of water
2. Observe what happens
3. Cover the measuring cylinder and shake to mix the oil and the water together
4. Let the cylinder stand and observe again
5. Explain to a partner why you think this happens

by sieving out the tiny plankton from the water that they take into their mouths.

Each species is specifically adapted to match the prey animals that it feeds on. Here are some examples:

- Horn sharks eat shellfish like crabs and so they have flattened teeth for crushing.
- Sand tiger sharks catch smaller fish to eat, so they need sharp pointed thin teeth that can spike and stick into the bodies of the slippery fish.
- Wobbegongs have flattened, camouflaged bodies so that they blend in with the seabed where they live.

The most famous and the most dangerous sharks are the great whites. They can grow to over 6 m long and weigh over 3200 kg, and usually the females are bigger than the males. The brain of the great white shark is only the size of your fist, so they are unable to learn very much during their lifetime and most of their behaviour is instinctive.

When hunting, they swim along the seabed listening for sounds and smelling the water as they move. The body is dark above and light below, and this makes it very difficult for their victims to see them.

Sound travels better through the water than it does through the air, so sharks can hear their prey from hundreds of metres away. Nostrils above the mouth constantly draw in water to 'sniff' and detect the presence of chemicals. Their sense of smell is very well developed: they can detect one drop of blood in 100 litres of water.

The great white is the only known species of shark to stick its head out of the water, but scientists don't know the reason why it does this. Maybe it is looking for prey or sniffing the air.

When a possible meal has been detected, the shark moves a little closer to investigate. Sensory pits over the face and body can detect vibrations in the water and identify where the prey is. The sensory pits lead into tubes that contain jelly, which ripples when there are vibrations in the water. Fish, a bird that has landed on the water, or maybe a swimmer struggling in the sea, might be the cause of the vibrations.

The closer the shark gets to its prey, the more it starts to rely on its eyes to see how far away it is and the best way to attack.

Great whites attack from below, moving very quickly and with force. When striking, they often close their eyes to protect them, so instead of seeing, they rely on pores on the snout, which can detect tiny electrical signals in the muscles of the prey animal. This information keeps them on track for a successful strike.

Sharks cannot chew, only bite and swallow. The bite of a great white is powerful enough to bend a steel bar; their jaw is 300 times more powerful than a human's. The mouth is lined with several rows of triangular shaped teeth with a saw-edge that is as sharp as a razor. Each tooth is approximately $7\frac{1}{2}$ cm long and is as hard as steel. The shark has about

3000 teeth at any one time. The teeth are arranged in rows, but the great white just uses the first two rows and the others grow forward to replace teeth that are lost or broken. A shark will have 20 000 teeth during its lifetime.

When the mouth is opened, the front rows of teeth reach forward. The prey is clamped in the jaws, then the shark twists and turns its whole body, violently thrashing to tear the animal apart into pieces that are small enough to swallow. A number of sharks can be found trying to feed on the same prey animal, resulting in a feeding frenzy as the large bodies twist and writhe in the water.

Great whites have enormous appetites and will eat when they can. The bulk of their diet is made up of fast-moving fish like tuna and swordfish, but they also feed on crabs, dolphins, other sharks, seals and sea lions, turtles and whales. In addition, they scavenge on dead animals and birds, and have been known to eat almost anything that they find, such as bottles, cans, clothes, floating buoys, and wood. Many strange things have been found in the stomach of a great white shark when it has been caught and opened up.

No point in trying to bite back!

7 Lay out six metre-long rules across the floor to see the size of an average great white shark.

8 Draw diagrams to show how particles are arranged in liquids and gases. Use these diagrams to explain to a partner why sound travels better through the water than it does through the air.

9 Bearing in mind that sharks can smell blood in minute amounts, you are going to test your ability to see red food dye in water. Work in groups.

You will need:
- container that holds 5 litres, e.g. large bucket
- 1 litre (1000 cm^3) measuring cylinder
- graduated 100 cm^3 beaker
- 2 small plain beakers
- red food dye
- pipette
- sheet of white paper
- tissues

This is what you do:

1 Measure out 5 litres of water into the container

2 Measure 100 cm^3 of water into the graduated beaker. With the pipette, add 3 drops of red food dye and stir. Rinse and empty the pipette

3 Half-fill the first plain beaker with water and place it on the white paper

4 Pipette 10 cm^3 of the red dye mixture into the container and stir

5 Half-fill the second plain beaker with liquid from the container, dry the outside and place it on the paper

6 Compare it with the beaker of water. Can you see the red colour? If not, empty the second beaker back into the container. Then repeat steps 4, 5 and 6 until you can see the colour

7 Compare with other groups the amount of dye mixture you added to the container in order to see the red colour

Sharks and humans

Sharks are probably the most frightening predators on the planet, yet they are not the biggest animals. Elephants, rhinoceros and many whales are bigger. The records also show that they don't kill many people. More people die from wasp and bee stings, or in car accidents, than they do from shark attacks. There are less than one hundred shark attacks on people reported each year. Interestingly, men are ten times more likely to be attacked than women, but scientists are not sure of the reasons why. On average, three people die out of every ten shark attacks and this is usually through loss of blood. Some people, however, have been swallowed whole.

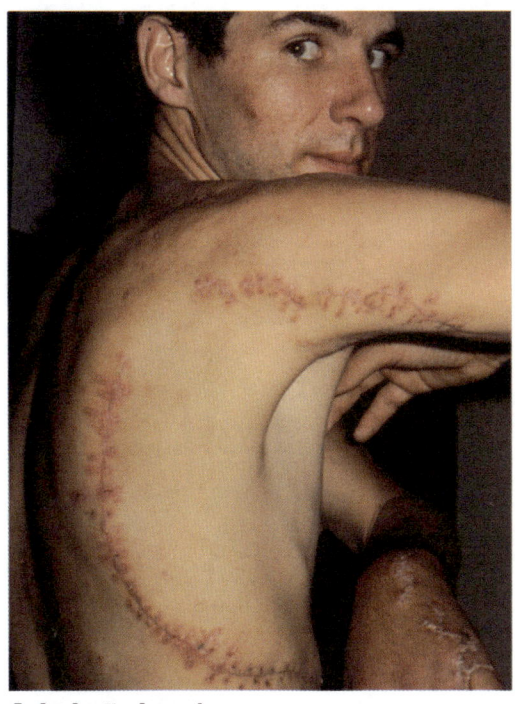

A shark-attack survivor.

The only safe way to observe great white sharks in their natural habitat is from a cage.

Sharks themselves have very little to fear – only other sharks and humans. Millions of sharks are caught every year for food, other products and for sport. The fins of sharks are often cut off and the rest of the shark is thrown back into the water to die. This is known as 'finning' and the fin is used to make shark fin soup. In the past, sailors used to use the rough skin from sharks to scrub the wooden decks of their ships. Nowadays, the skin is used to make belts, shoes and bags. The teeth of sharks are made into ornaments, weapons and jewellery. The oil from the liver is used to make health pills and anti-wrinkle cream, but in the past it was a fuel for lamps.

There is still a lot that we do not know about sharks, partly because they are difficult and dangerous animals to study. Researchers observing shark behaviour need to dress in a diving suit made of chain mail before being lowered into the sea inside a strong steel cage. They can also carry a POD (Protective Oceanic Device), which is powered by batteries to create an electrical field around the cage that, hopefully, confuses the sharks so they do not attack.

25

Studies have shown that shark numbers are under threat from over-fishing and pollution. In 1993, finning was banned in the USA, and Canada followed suit a year later. Great white sharks are also protected along the coasts of South Africa. Although they are fearsome predators, it would be a great loss if they disappeared altogether from our seas.

Disappearing sharks

Biologists at a university in Canada have been studying the records kept by fishermen of the Atlantic Ocean. The fishermen have to make a note of all the fish they catch, even those that they catch by mistake.

The records show that, apart from one species of shark that lives in the Atlantic, all the others have been dropping in numbers because of over-fishing. The scientists estimate that since 1986 the sizes of the populations have dropped by the amounts shown in the table.

Species of shark	Percentage drop in numbers
Blue	60
Great White	79
Hammerhead	89
Mako	20–25
Thresher	80
Tiger	65

Since sharks are the top predators, their disappearance would have a major impact on the rest of the food web in the Atlantic Ocean.

10 Brainstorm with a partner reasons why you think men are ten times more likely to be attacked by sharks than women. Compare your list with another group.

11 Draw a bar chart to show the percentage drop in the numbers of sharks in the Atlantic Ocean since 1986. Put the sharks in order, starting with the population that has decreased the most.

12 Visit these websites to find out more about sharks:
www.pelagic.org
www.sharks.org
www.ucmp.berkeley.edu/vertebrates/Doug/shark.html
www.sharkresearch.com

This website has an interactive camera in a shark tank:
marinelab.sarasota.fl.us

This website has recent data on shark attacks around the world:
www.flmnh.ufl.edu/fish/sharks/statistics/statistics.htm

Once you have lots of information, produce a PowerPoint presentation explaining why sharks are such successful predators.

Review

Use the information you have learnt in this chapter to solve the crossword puzzle on the following page.

Across

3, 7 Battery powered machine used by divers to deter sharks (10, 7 and 6)

9 The word used to describe how the shape of a shark's teeth is suited to their use (7)

10 Cutting off the shark fin to make soup (7)

11 The fins at the side of a shark's body (8)

12, 14 The largest shark (5, 5)

13 The type of pits on the shark's body that detect vibrations in the water (7)

Down

1 The fin on the back of a shark (6)

2 The design of the shark's body that reduces drag as it moves through the water (11)

4 Describes a skeleton made of gristle (13)

5 The egg sac of a shark (8, 5)

6 The group of fish that sharks belong to (13)

8 Meat-eaters, like sharks (10)

Chapter summary

In this chapter you have found out that:
- Sharks are cartilaginous fish that have been on the planet for millions of years.
- Their streamlined shape is an adaptation for fast and powerful swimming.
- Their sense organs allow them to detect prey animals from many metres away.
- Their teeth are adapted to the prey animals that they eat.

27

Behaviour of wild animals

Introduction

In this chapter, we find out what scientists have discovered from studying the behaviour of animals.

- The behaviour of animals can help us to classify them into groups.
- Investigating the behaviour responses of animals is difficult to do scientifically.
- There are two main categories of behaviour – innate and learned.

Work with a partner. For each of the animals listed, think of a characteristic behaviour. For instance, dogs will fetch and bring back a ball that has been thrown for them.

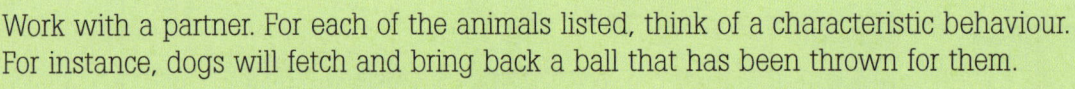
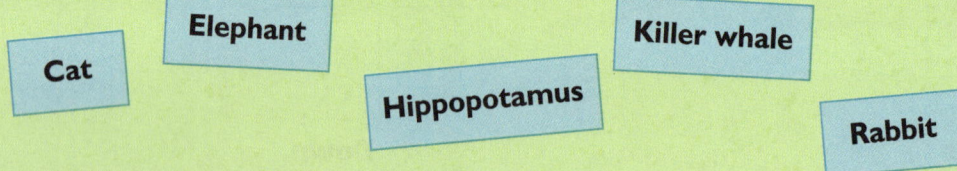

Try to explain the reasons for these behaviours.

Why study behaviour?

Studying the way animals behave really helps scientists to understand them. They try to find out what the animals do in response to particular stimuli. A stimulus is simply something that triggers off a specific behaviour. Studies of behaviour provide information that helps us work out the ways in which organisms interact with their environment.

Patterns in behaviour can also provide clues about which animals are related to each other. Animals that behave in similar ways are likely to be quite closely related. Animals that behave very differently are less likely to be closely related. Studying behaviour is therefore another way of helping scientists to classify animals into groups.

For example, human beings use more tools than any other animal on the planet. By tools, we mean anything that helps them to do particular jobs. Second on the list of tool users is the chimpanzee. Chimps use sticks, grass, leaves and stones as tools. Stones are used like a hammer and anvil to crack open nuts. The sticks can be used in all sorts of ways – attacking other animals, for poking into holes to collect ants and termites for a tasty snack, or as a toy to tease other chimps with. Leaves can be used like a sponge to soak up water that is then squeezed into the mouth for a drink. Chimps also use leaves to wash themselves. Anyone watching the way chimpanzees behave will be reminded of themselves. This isn't very surprising when you realise that chimps are our closest living relatives.

Like humans, chimps are tool users.

Ways of studying behaviour

Studying the behaviour of wild animals is surprisingly difficult to do. Normally, scientists investigate things by carrying out controlled experiments in the laboratory. They change one thing at a time (the independent variable) to measure how it affects something else (the dependent variable). To make it a fair test, everything else is kept the same throughout the experiment. You will have done plenty of experiments like this in your science lessons.

If you do this with wild animals, however, you take them out of their natural habitat, which means they might not behave the way they normally do. If instead you go out into their natural habitat to observe their behaviour, it is difficult to know what stimulus they are responding to, as there are so many variables affecting them at any one time.

Scientists therefore use both methods. Researching animals in the wild can take many years of close observation and recording before any definite patterns in their behaviour begin to emerge.

Jane Goodall

Jane Goodall is famous for her studies of chimpanzees in Africa and the many great discoveries she has made about their behaviour. She first went to Africa in 1957, and since then she has written very many articles and letters about her time with the chimpanzees. The following is an extract from a letter she wrote to Prince Bernhard of the Netherlands in 1983.

> *Since you left Tanzania I have made a two-week visit to Gombe where I found the work progressing very well, although somewhat hampered by heavy rain. It is always so fantastic to actually get back into the field and be with the chimps for a while after spending so much time poring over the data and writing up the results. The termite fishing season was in full swing and it was fascinating to watch the techniques of the different infants and juveniles as they tried to capture the termites. There is quite a marked individual difference in age at which they start to concentrate and are able to manipulate the grasses and stems in a satisfactory and productive manner.*

From Jane Goodall, *Beyond Innocence*

Nowadays, a wide range of technical equipment can be used to help with these observations. Video cameras can be set up in a nest or den to closely observe the behaviour of parents with their offspring. Infra-red cameras can be used to capture the hunting behaviour of a pack of hyenas during the night. Tracking devices linked to satellite systems can be used to follow the movements of a pod of migrating whales through the oceans. Microphones can pick up the songs of birds in a forest and the sounds can be analysed by a computer to help us understand how they communicate with each other.

All of the work carried out so far has helped us to realise that behaviour can be divided into two main types: innate behaviour and learned behaviour.

1 Copy and complete the following table:

Technique for studying behaviour	Advantages	Disadvantages
Controlled experiments in the lab		
Observations in the wild		

Innate behaviour

This type of behaviour is built in, meaning that the animal is born with it. It enables the animal to know the difference between harmful things and useful things and so is essential for survival. A particular stimulus should always produce a particular response, because it is 'wired into' the nervous system. The genes control innate behaviour.

There are 4 types of innate behaviour.

Reflexes

Vertebrate animals have reflexes that help to protect them from harm. If you touch something hot, even before you have time to think about it you will withdraw your hand so that you don't burn yourself. If you move into bright light, your pupils will contract so that less light enters your eyes. This protects them, since too much light would damage the retina at the back of the eye and you could eventually go blind. You might have seen doctors on television checking this reflex in the eyes of unconscious patients.

If you had to think about doing things like this, your responses would be too slow and you would be harmed. Reflexes happen fast and you are born with them.

2 You are going to test reflexes.

You will need:
- a partner
- metre ruler

This is what you do:

1 Check the pupil reflex of your partner. Look at their eyes carefully to see the size of the pupils. Ask them to cover up one eye with their hand for 30 seconds before quickly moving the hand away. What happens to the size of the pupil?

2 Check the reflex in your partner's arms. Hold the metre ruler so that the zero mark is at the bottom, next to your partner's fingers. Drop the ruler so that your partner has to catch it as quickly as possible. The faster they react, the smaller the number on the ruler where they catch it. You can only do this test once because otherwise your partner will be using information they have learnt from the first test to help them improve their reaction

3 Check the knee reflex of your partner. Ask them to sit with one leg crossed over the knee of the other. This leg should be dangling and not touching the floor. Find the base of their kneecap and tap here gently. If you tap them just on the right spot, their leg will automatically kick out

Taxes

In the type of behaviour called a taxis (plural: taxes), animals move their whole body either towards or away from a particular stimulus. The table shows a few examples of taxes:

Stimulus	Example
Chemicals	Bacteria move towards food, attracted by the chemicals.
	Mosquitoes move away from insect repellant because of the chemicals it contains.
Light	*Euglena* (a single-celled organism) moves towards the light.
	Woodlice move away from the light because they prefer to be in dark places where it is more likely to be damp.

3 Investigate how woodlice behave to the stimulus of light.

You will need:
- choice chamber
- black paper
- sample of woodlice
- lamp
- stopwatch

This is what you do:

1 Set up the choice chamber as shown in the diagram
2 Gently put the woodlice into the chamber through the hole in the centre
3 Leave the woodlice for a few minutes to adjust to their new surroundings
4 Switch on the lamp and start the stopwatch
5 After 5 minutes, count and record how many of the woodlice are in the light and how many are in the dark
6 Repeat after another 5 minutes

Choice chamber seen from the top

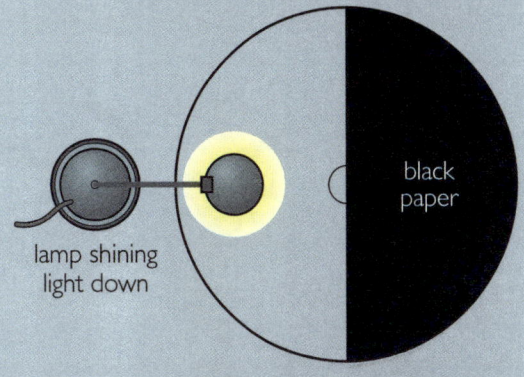

Choice chamber seen from the side

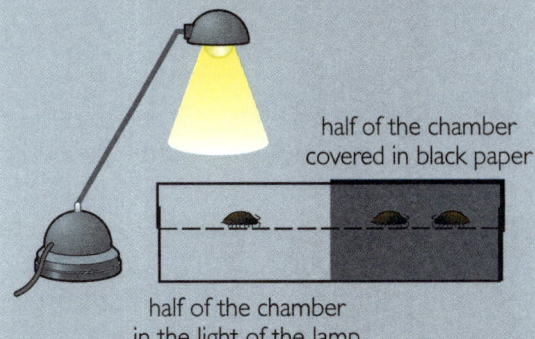

4 Answer these questions about the woodlice investigation:

a What is the independent variable?
b Why is a sample used instead of just one woodlouse?
c List the variables that need to be kept constant for a fair test.
d Why are the woodlice put into the centre of the chamber?
e What do your results tell you about which side of the chamber the woodlice prefer?
f How can the results from this experiment be made more reliable?

Kineses

In this type of behaviour, animals change the speed at which they are moving when a stimulus gets stronger. For example, the centimetre-high Hydra catches food with its tentacles. It slowly moves these tentacles in the water all the time, but when it detects that food is nearby, the movement of the tentacles speeds up to draw the food closer to its mouth.

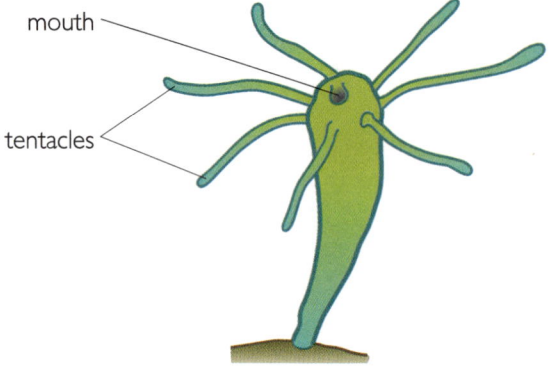

Instincts

Instincts are patterns in behaviour – a whole set of ready-made responses to a particular stimulus. Animals need instincts to help them survive, and are particularly important when the animals don't live for very long. If they aren't looked after by their parents when young, they need to be born knowing instinctively how to find or catch their food, how to defend a territory or how to court a mate. All animals that are nurtured when young know instinctively how to look after their own offspring.

Really wild animals

Sometimes people forget that animals are wild and can behave in an unpredictable way. The following is a report about attacks on people by a badger.

> A quiet corner of rural England was recovering yesterday after a bruising encounter with Boris the badger.
>
> Five people were put in hospital and two police officers were sent scurrying for cover after the bad-tempered creature went on a 48-hour rampage through Evesham in Worcestershire.
>
> As the last victim returned from hospital yesterday after having skin grafts to his legs and an arm, residents described Boris's arrival as being like a scene from a horror film…
>
> The badger's rampage eventually ended on Saturday when he was caught under a crate by Michael Weaver, chairman of the Worcestershire Badger Society.
>
> Afterwards Mr Weaver said that the badger's behaviour was unprecedented. 'I have never heard of anything like this in 24 years of work with badgers throughout the UK.'
>
> From an article by Sam Lister in *The Times*, Wednesday 14 May 2003

5 a As a class, brainstorm reasons why you think the badger attacked the people in the news story.

b As a class, brainstorm what should have been done with the badger after it was caught. Once you have a list of all the possibilities, hold a class vote to decide, with reasons, which you would choose from your list.

Learned behaviour

When animals learn, they adapt their behaviour and the changes made are based on what they remember from a previous experience. This means that animals must have a memory if they are going to learn. Memory can be divided into two types: short-term memory that only lasts for a few minutes; and long-term memory that lasts much longer, maybe years.

Scientists have discovered that chemicals in the brain are linked with memory. Experiments show that a rat can be taught to carry out a particular task, for example, solving a maze to find food at the other end. Once the rat can do the task, it is killed and its brain is removed and ground into a liquid. This liquid can then be injected into another rat. The new rat can then solve the maze in a much shorter time, showing that chemicals in the brain liquid have, somehow, carried some memory of the task.

However, these sorts of experiments only tell us a little about what is going on in the brain, so scientists are still very unsure about how different animals learn. There seem to be many different ways that learning happens. Scientists have divided them into a number of different types, as follows.

Imprinting

This is a behaviour that is learnt by young animals. They associate themselves with another animal and copy their behaviour. Imprinting happens at a particular time in a young animal's life, usually when it is still in the nest or den. This means that the young animal is most likely to imprint on a parent, often the mother. Once this behaviour has been learnt, it is very difficult to change.

Imprinting is extremely important for survival of the young. They quickly learn what their mother looks like so that they can go to her for food, protection and warmth. Later in life, they use what they have learnt to recognise possible mates.

The first scientist to investigate imprinting was Konrad Lorenz in the 1930s. He made observations of chickens, ducks and geese in farmyards. He even managed to get chicks to imprint on him so that they followed behind him when he walked.

Research into memory

In 2003, researchers at the Massachusetts Institute of Technology experimented to find out which parts of our brains are involved in forming memories. Volunteers were put into a magnetic resonance imaging (MRI) scanner that can form images of the brain. Each volunteer was given 400 words to read. Half the volunteers were asked to try to remember the words by thinking of a picture that connects with the word. The other half were asked to remember the words by reading them backwards. The researchers were able to get images of inside the brains as the volunteers were doing this.

The next day, the volunteers were put back in the scanner and shown more words, some of them the same as the words they were asked to remember. They told the researchers whether or not they remembered each word.

From the data they collected, the research scientists were able to conclude that one part of the brain remembers a word itself, but that a different part of the brain is involved if the person thinks of a picture to go with the word.

Habituation

Again, this is behaviour learnt by young animals to help them to understand the habitat they are living in. Over time they learn to ignore a particular stimulus – they become 'habituated' to it. This is because they realise that they do not need to respond to that stimulus as it doesn't give them any reward (e.g. food), nor does it harm them in any way.

Farmers understand habituation when they see that birds learn to ignore the scarecrows they have put in the fields to protect their crops.

Associative learning

Conditioned reflexes

Conditioned reflexes are usually reflexes of innate behaviours, but they can become associated with another stimulus. For example, birds instinctively know that bees and wasps can sting, but they learn to avoid catching all insects that show a black and yellow striped pattern. The birds associate the colours with the sting and do not attempt to eat these insects.

A famous Russian scientist called Ivan Pavlov carried out experiments on dogs to find out about conditioned reflexes. When dogs are shown a bowl of food, their natural reflex is to start to salivate: they start dribbling and licking their lips. Pavlov trained dogs to show this as a conditioned reflex. He rang a bell at the same time as presenting a bowl of food to the dog. After a while, just ringing the bell would get the dog to start salivating. The dog had associated the sound of the bell with the bowl of food.

Your own pets at home might do the same sort of thing. If they hear you opening a tin of food they might come running because they think that the tin will mean food for them.

Humans learn a lot through conditioned reflexes too – what do you do as soon as you hear a bell ring for example?

Trial-and-error learning

This is where animals learn a particular type of behaviour just by chance. They associate what they have done with a particular stimulus. If they are rewarded, they will do the same thing again and again. If they are punished, they will learn avoid that behaviour.

Exploratory learning

This type of behaviour has no immediate benefit for the animal, but it may turn out to be important in the future. For example, if mice are moved into a new burrow they will explore to learn their way around. They might need this in the future, for example when they have to escape from predators who have got into the burrow.

Insight

This type of behaviour is considered to be the most advanced. It involves animals using behaviours that they have learnt before in a brand new situation. Animals can be observed seemingly 'thinking' about what to do and scientists assume that this involves some level of thought, like the way that humans think.

Wolfgang Kohler experimented with chimpanzees that were kept in a cage. The chimps were given boxes to play with, so they spent time exploring the boxes and learning what happened to them if they moved them, stood on them, picked them up and so on. Kohler then hung bananas, out of reach, from the roof of the cage. After a time, the chimps worked out that they could stack the boxes on top of each other and then climb up to reach the bananas. They were associating what they had learnt about the boxes with the reward that the bananas would bring them – this is described as 'insight'.

6 You are going to investigate how quickly another class can learn how to solve a maze. The students in the class that you test must not have seen the information that follows.

You will need:
- photocopies of a maze you have drawn (like the types you see in a puzzle book)
- sweets (as rewards)
- cleaning cloths (as punishment)
- stopwatches

This is what you do:

1 Divide the class you are investigating into 5 groups. Test each group individually, without the others seeing what happens

2 Group 1 is the control group. Just let them do the maze but don't tell them that you are timing them. Record the results

3 Group 2 should be told that they will be timed while they solve the maze

4 Group 3 are the exploratory learning group. Give them 30 seconds to look at the maze before you time how long it takes them to solve it

5 Group 4 are the positive reward group. Tell them that the fastest person to solve the maze will be given sweets as a reward

6 Group 5 are the negative punishment group. Tell them that the last person to solve the maze will have to clean all the desks in the classroom

7 Record all the results

7 Answer these questions about the maze investigation.

a What was the reason for the control group?

b For each group's results, calculate the mean (average) time to complete the maze, and the range of the times (shortest time – longest time).

c Display these results in a chart similar to this:

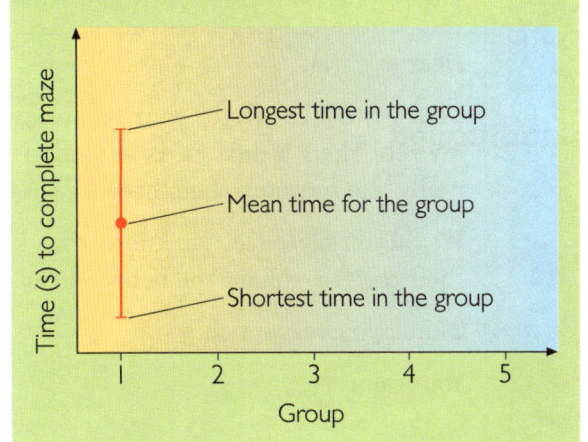

d Which group took the shortest time to complete the maze? (Compare the mean times.)

e Which group took the longest time to complete the maze? (Compare the mean times.)

f Which group has the greatest range in times to complete the maze?

g Give possible reasons to explain these results.

h What was the sample size in each group?

i Why did you test a sample of people and not just one person?

j How could the results from this experiment be made more reliable?

Web Links

Visit these websites to find out more about the behaviour of animals:

www.bbc.co.uk/nature/animals
www.bbc.co.uk/beasts/evidence/prog1/page5_2.shtml
www.bbc.co.uk/nature/animals/pets/testyourpet/science.shtml
www.bbc.co.uk/nature/animals/mammals/explore/print/instincts.shtml

Review

Write a reply to this letter from a zookeeper:

> Dear scientist,
>
> I am writing to ask for your help. A group of chimpanzees has recently arrived in my zoo. Their behaviour is very interesting and, of course, the visitors to the zoo really like to watch them because they are so similar to us.
>
> Would you please let me know what I should write on the display board outside their cage to explain the behaviour of the chimps to the visiting public.
>
> Thank you very much.
>
> Yours sincerely,
>
> *Mr Fide*

Chapter summary

In this chapter you have found out that:
- Studying animal behaviour helps scientists to classify them into groups.
- Behaviour can be studied under controlled conditions in the lab or through close observation in the wild.
- Innate and learned behaviour are the two major types of behaviour.

Responding to the seasons

Introduction

In this chapter, we look at some of the ways in which organisms are adapted to seasonal changes in their environment.

- Physical and biological changes occur within an environment according to the four different seasons of the year.
- Organisms must adapt to these changes in order to survive within their habitats.
- Plants and animals have a variety of adaptations to cope with these changes in their habitats.

The diagrams show the seasons in Britain. Work with a partner to copy and complete the following table using the diagrams and your own knowledge to help you.

Season	Physical conditions	Biological conditions
Spring	e.g. Warm temperature	e.g. Spring flowers grow from bulbs
Summer		
Autumn		
Winter		

37

Adaptations to survival

As the Earth orbits round the Sun during the year, different countries of the world experience different conditions. The different light levels and the temperature changes bring about a whole range of other varying physical conditions. These in turn affect the organisms that are living in particular places (the biological conditions).

Around the Equator, there are two seasons: a dry, cool season and a wet, hot season. Further from the Equator, there are the four seasons like the ones we experience in Britain.

Organisms have developed a number of adaptations to cope with these changes in their environment. They need ways to survive the conditions that are difficult, such as very low temperatures or drought. They also need to take advantage of the conditions during the year that are more suitable to life, such as increased light levels and abundant supplies of food.

The ability of organisms to adapt to the conditions determines which species are found in particular habitats around the world.

1 As a class, brainstorm all the ways in which your life is different in winter from the way it is in summer and how these changes are important for your survival.

2 As a class, brainstorm all the ways in which birds cope with winter conditions and how each adaptation helps them to survive.

3 Set up a bird feeding station in a suitable place in your school grounds. Investigate how many different types of birds visit the feeding station, and then record whether the numbers depend on the type of food you have put out for them.

This is what you need:
- a variety of different bird foods
- a bird table or hanging bird feeder

This is what you do:

1 For the bird foods, visit your local pet shop or gardening centre for advice, making sure that you do not feed the birds anything that is unsuitable

2 Set up your feeding station in a safe place where you can easily view it without frightening the birds and leave out a variety of foods and some water

3 Be patient; it will take the birds some time to realise that there is food available for them and that it is safe for them to visit

4 Make regular observations, at a distance, noting the date, time, weather conditions and the number of birds that visit

5 Clean the feeding station and replace the food regularly

6 Once you have collected sufficient data, decide on a suitable way to display it

7 Now experiment with one particular food at a time. Leave out just one type of food and observe to see if there are any changes in the numbers and types of birds that visit

- Is it possible to match a particular type of bird to the food that you have left out?

How plants survive seasonal changes

In Britain, there are many different species of plants. They can be grouped into one of three different categories, depending on the time it takes them to go through their life cycle. The life cycle of a plant begins with the germination of a seed, followed by growth so that the leaves can photosynthesise and make food for the plant. When the plant has enough energy, it moves on to the third stage of its life cycle, which is to reproduce and make seeds of its own that are then dispersed.

- Annual plants complete this life cycle within one year. The seeds germinate in the spring when the temperature starts to rise. The plant can then make maximum use of the increased light levels during the summer to grow quickly and develop flowers. Pollinating insects are also present during the summer months, so an insect-pollinated plant can reproduce. In the autumn, the plant dies, but the seeds survive the winter with a store of food inside ready to supply energy for germination when spring comes round again.

- Biennials need two years to complete their life cycle. During the first year, the plant germinates from a seed and then grows as much as it can in the summer. The food that is made by photosynthesis is changed into starch and stored underground over winter. In the second year, this food store is used to grow a stem and new leaves in the spring, and then the plant reproduces in the summer. The seeds survive the winter with a store of food inside them.

- Perennials are plants that repeat their life cycle year after year. Each year they grow bigger until they reach their maximum height and die of old age. Some of the food they make during the summer months is stored to help them survive the winter months when the light levels and temperature are too low for efficient photosynthesis.

Deciduous trees are perennials that lose their leaves in the autumn to help them survive the winter. They do this because their leaves have a large surface area from which they can lose water very quickly. In the winter, they may not be able to replace this water if it is frozen in the soil.

Bacteria, fungi and small animals like worms feed on dead leaves and break them down into their basic minerals. Their dead remains and droppings put these minerals back into the soil. This replaces the minerals in the soil, and plants can use them during the spring of the following year to improve their growth.

4 Work with a partner and use books in your school library to find examples of plants that belong to each of the categories: annuals, biennials, and perennials.

5 Investigate the conditions needed for leaf litter to decompose.

You will need:
- leaf litter
- balance
- net material
- elastic bands
- measuring cylinder
- fridge
- lamp
- heater
- plastic gloves

⚠ *Wear the plastic gloves and wash your hands to avoid spreading germs.*

This is what you do:

1 Wearing plastic gloves, measure on the balance 6 equal masses of leaf litter

2 Dry one sample of leaf litter by leaving it on top of a heater

3. Add 10 cm³ of water, measured in the cylinder, onto a second sample of leaf litter
4. Cut out 6 equal squares of net material, large enough for the leaf litter to fit inside
5. Put each of the 6 samples of leaf litter into one of the squares of net material and fold up the edges to form 6 bags
6. Secure the tops of the bags with the elastic bands
7. Leave the dried leaves, wet leaves and a third bag of leaves in the same place in the science lab
8. Put the fourth bag in the fridge
9. Put the fifth bag under a lamp
10. Put the last bag on top of the heater
11. Predict which of the bags has the most suitable conditions for the leaves to be decomposed and explain why you think this
12. Check the bags once a week, wearing plastic gloves each time, to compare the rate of decay

6 Answer these questions about the leaf litter investigations.
(Sc1)

a Describe the 6 different conditions the leaves have been left in.

b List the variables that have been kept constant for a fair test.

c Describe the conditions that are difficult to control for a fair test.

d Use the results to explain whether your prediction was correct.

Hibernating animals

Hibernation is a technique used by animals to survive the cold weather of the winter months when there is very little food available.

Some animals enter into a true hibernation; this is a very deep sleep when their body temperature drops close to the temperature of their surroundings. The heart rate, breathing rate and growth all slow down during the time they are asleep. Examples include dormice, hamsters, hedgehogs and shrews.

Other hibernating animals become dormant, which means they sleep but can wake up periodically during the winter period. Examples include frogs, lizards, newts, snakes, toads and tortoises.

During the summer and autumn, hibernating animals build up stores of fat from the food they eat, and some gather food to leave in their burrow for when they wake up. The layers of insulating fat reduce heat loss from their bodies while they sleep. They also build a special burrow or nest to hibernate in that is, as far as possible, insulated against the cold. The animal curls itself up in order to reduce its surface area and so loses as little heat as possible during the hibernation or dormancy period. The stores of fat are used up steadily over the winter months.

Hibernation is brought on by a decrease in the temperature and light levels. It is believed by scientists that a chemical in the blood controls when an animal will go into hibernation. To investigate this, experiments have been carried out on squirrels. Blood from a hibernating squirrel was injected into a squirrel that was not hibernating. In less than two days, the second squirrel had also gone into hibernation.

When the winter comes to an end, the animal becomes active again quite quickly. Heat is generated to warm the body and restore its normal active temperature. The brain, heart and lungs receive this heat first, and then it reaches the rest of the body.

Aestivation

Aestivation is very similar to hibernation but is a technique used by some animals that live in the desert to survive severe periods of drought. When very little water is available there is also very little food, so it is difficult for animals to survive. Aestivating animals slow down their breathing rate because every time they breathe out they lose water vapour.

7 Work with a partner to research an animal that hibernates. Produce a poster or PowerPoint presentation to help you feed back the information you have found to the rest of the class. Visit these websites to help you with your research:
- www.sciencemadesimple.com/animals.html
- www.pbs.org/wgbh/nova/satoyama/hibernation.html
- www.expage.com/page/mrsgwinter2

Migrating animals

Migration is another technique that animals use to survive throughout the changing conditions of the year. For example, they move to areas where there is more food available to them, where the temperature is higher or where it is safe to breed.

Animals that migrate include whales, butterflies and birds.

In Britain, the arrival of spring brings with it birds such as swifts, swallows, chiffchaffs and sedge warblers. What is amazing is how they find their way, often returning to the same nesting site year after year. It is also amazing how far some of these migrating animals actually travel. The Arctic tern flies nearly the whole length of the world in its migration, spending the winter in the Antarctic and then flying 11 000 miles to the far north of America and Europe.

Review

Work with a partner to decide what would be a suitable question for each of these answers:

a The organisms living in a particular habitat at a particular time.

b The point when a plant begins to grow from a seed.

c To reduce water loss, as the roots may not be able to absorb water from the frozen soil.

d By having layers of fat, lining the nest or burrow and curling up to reduce their surface area.

e When animals and birds go to another part of the world that has more suitable conditions for survival at that time of year.

Chapter summary

In this chapter you have found out that:
- Organisms must adapt to the seasonal changes of their habitat if they are to survive.
- Organisms are adapted in different ways to survive low or high temperatures, lack of water and lack of food.
- The organisms that are found in a habitat will be those that are adapted to the physical and biological conditions of that particular habitat at that particular time of the year.

Animal adaptations

Introduction

In this chapter, we look at a few examples of how animals are adapted to survive in the habitat in which they live.

- Organisms are adapted to the time of the day during which they are active.
- Organisms are adapted to the physical conditions of their habitat.
- Organisms are adapted to the way in which they feed.
- The adaptations of an organism help it to survive in a particular habitat, but they may not be suited to another habitat.

As a class, brainstorm all the things that animals need to survive.

Why are adaptations so varied?

All organisms are adapted to their habitat in order to survive. These adaptations vary depending on the physical conditions of the habitat, such as temperature and the availability of light and water. There are very many different habitats around the world and organisms have adapted in very many different ways to suit the conditions they live in.

Organisms also have adaptations to best suit their position in the food chain.

1 Copy and complete the following table, adding at least one extra habitat of your own choice.

Habitat	Physical conditions
Desert	Very high temperatures during the day, low temperatures at night. Shortage of water.
The ground of a British woodland	
The canopy of a tropical rainforest	
Arctic Ocean	

2 Organisms are adapted to their position in the food chain. Put these terms into the correct order and join them with arrows to form a food chain:

Top predator   Primary consumer   Secondary consumer   Producer

3 Identify these birds and match each one to the correct picture of their feet. Try to explain why their feet are adapted in this way.

Arctic fox

Red fox

for its prey to see it. In Britain, a white fox would be far more visible than the red fox for most of the year.

4 Work with a partner to decide, apart from the colour of the fur, the adaptations of the Arctic fox for survival in its habitat.

Camouflage

Animals are often coloured so that they blend in to their surroundings. Predators are camouflaged to make it harder for their prey to spot them. Prey are camouflaged to make it harder for their predators to see them.

Frogs, for example, can be very difficult to spot until they move. They are brown, green, yellow and black with whitish areas underneath. This dappled pattern helps to camouflage frogs against their background. Frogs can also change their colour slightly. In the skin they have cells containing pigment (colour). By expanding or contracting these cells, the skin of the frog can be made darker or lighter to help it blend in even more.

The Arctic fox has white fur to camouflage it against the snow. This makes it more difficult

At first sight, zebras seem to have the worst camouflage design you have ever seen! Their black and white stripes stand out clearly against the green/yellow background of the grass plains of Africa where they live. The usefulness of their design can be understood, however, when you see a herd of zebra moving together. The stripes blend into each other so that it is difficult to see where one animal ends and the next one begins. Their predators need to spot and isolate an individual in order to kill it. The stripes are therefore a camouflage that helps to protect zebras by confusing their predators.

The masters of disguise in the animal kingdom are the insects. Stick insects immediately spring to mind, looking exactly like small twigs. When resting, they hold the front part of their bodies perfectly straight out from the twig that they are attached to, in order to make themselves even more difficult to spot.

The lower 'twig' is the stick insect, hanging upside down from the upper twig.

There is even a type of beetle in Brazil that can look exactly like a bird dropping to avoid being eaten!

The orchid mantis is a predator that feeds on other insects. It has extended shapes on its body and legs that exactly match the petals of the orchid on which it lives. It is so difficult to spot that insects walk right up to it. When it attacks, its body can suddenly be seen, but by this time it is too late for the insect to escape and it becomes a meal.

5 Test the effectiveness of camouflage as a protection against being seen and caught.

You will need:
- green and red pipe cleaners
- stopwatch
- string

This is what you do:

1 Section off an area of your school field by creating a large square with the string

2 Divide the class into two groups. Those in the first group position the pipe cleaners within the square, equal numbers of each colour

3 Those in the second group then have a time limit to find and retrieve as many of the pipe cleaners as possible

4 Record how many pipe cleaners of each colour where found

5 Collect the remaining pipe cleaners

6 Swap the groups over and repeat

6 Calculate the percentage of green pipe cleaners found, and compare it to the percentage of red pipe cleaners found.

The orchid mantis consists of all the white structures, which are disguised to look like flower parts. Its head is lower right, and it grasps its prey by extending the spiked forelegs seen to the left of its head.

Catching prey

Predators have developed many adaptations to improve their chances of catching their prey. One adaptation involves the position of the eyes on the head. Some predators, for example birds of prey, have their eyes positioned at the front of the head. This gives the predators binocular vision, making it easier to judge distances and, therefore, to work out the distance of their prey and catch it. In addition, bird predators such as eagles have amazing eyesight, being able to spot a rabbit from 3000 metres away.

Other prey animals such as rabbits, have their eyes positioned at the sides of the head. This allows them to remain perfectly still whilst being able to look practically all round them on the look-out for predators.

The chameleon can actually move each of its eyes independently, so that one eye can be looking forwards, whilst the other looks backwards. This allows the chameleon to watch out for predators. When it wants to catch its own prey, however, it moves both eyes to point forwards so that it restores binocular vision and then can judge the distance it needs to extend its sticky tongue and grab its food.

Some hunters use both camouflage and a bait to attract their prey to them. The anglerfish so closely matches its surroundings on the seabed that it is almost invisible. From its head, however, extends a strange 'fishing rod'. As the rod dangles in the water it attracts fish towards it, tempted by the possibility of a meal. Little do they know that they are to be the meal when the anglerfish reveals itself and gobbles up the duped fish.

Other predators don't wait for their prey to come to them. Sea lion pups would seem to be safe from killer whales when they are huddled together on a beach, but the killer whale can perform a surprising trick. Swimming really fast towards the shore, the whale can come crashing onto the beach, hidden by the white froth of the waves. It grabs a pup in its mouth before turning and thrashing its body to get back into the water.

Nocturnal predators need specific adaptations to help them find their prey in the dark of night. Bats, although not blind, do not rely on their eyesight to catch the moths and other insects that they feed on. Instead, they send out high-pitched sounds that constantly bounce back as echoes when they hit objects. By listening to these echoes, the bats are able to work out the location of their prey.

7 Test how well you can judge distances with only one eye. You will need:
- partner
- pen with lid
- ball
- patch to cover one eye

This is what you do:

1. Cover one eye with the patch
2. Your partner holds a pen at arm's length away from you
3. You must try to put the lid on the pen
4. Swap the eye patch over to try with the other eye covered
5. Your partner then throws the ball towards you and you must try to catch it
6. Swap the eye patch round again and try with the other eye covered

- Was there a difference between looking with your left eye or your right eye?
- Was there a difference judging the distance of a stationary object or a moving object?

Poisons and stings

Animals use poisons and stings to both attack and kill their prey and as protection against being eaten themselves.

A jellyfish, known as the Portuguese man-of-war, uses deadly stinging tentacles to catch and kill its prey. The jellyfish can reach down over 2 metres from the top of its body, which floats on the surface of the water, to the end of the tentacles, which trail below the surface. The jellyfish does not swim, but instead drifts along in the currents of the Atlantic Ocean waiting for fish to swim past its tentacles. Any fish that do will be stung and quickly paralysed, so that they can be drawn towards the mouth and eaten. The poison in the sting is strong enough to kill a small child.

An amphibian that is famous for its chemical weapons is the poison arrow frog that lives in the rainforests of South America. The Indians living in the forests use this poison to their own advantage. They do not eat the frog, but instead they put the poison from its skin onto the tips of their arrows. They then use these arrows to hunt animals such as monkeys. The Indians need to be careful, because just 0.0001 g of the poison can kill a man.

Animals that have poisonous chemicals in their bodies to protect them need to advertise the fact. A predator needs to know to avoid them, otherwise it will only find out they are poisonous after it has eaten one! Animals with poisons and stings are, therefore, brightly coloured to warn off possible predators.

Mimicry

Yellow and black stripes on an insect seem to be a signal that is understood by humans and other animals. The stripes say about the insect: 'I can sting, so do not eat me.' Animals and children learn very quickly that bees, wasps and hornets should be avoided.

Other insects, however, have taken advantage of this colour-coded message. By displaying the bright colours that are normally only worn by stinging, poisonous insects, they can protect themselves from predators. These insects (and other animals that have the colouring of dangerous creatures) are known as mimics. They copy the warning colours, but are not actually capable of poisoning or stinging. The hoverfly is an example of a mimic.

Animals have many ways to protect themselves from predators and to ensure that they catch their prey.

Chameleon

Hoverfly

Portuguese man-of-war jellyfish

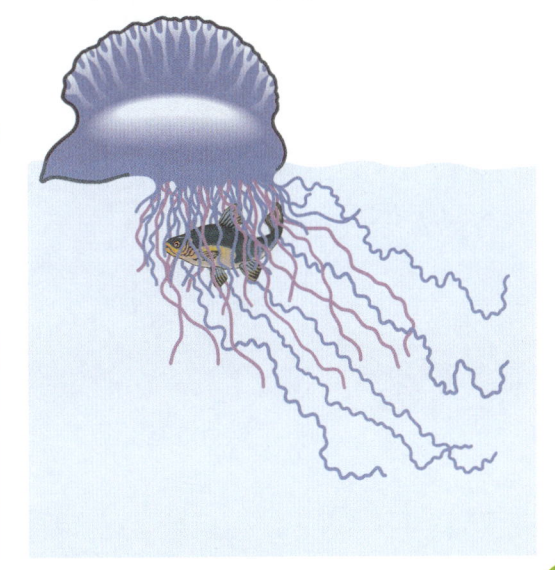

Anglerfish

Web Links

Visit these websites to find out more about camouflage:
www.thewildones.org/Animals/camo.html
www.howstuffworks.com/animal camouflage.htm
www.longhorn-cattle.com/camo.html
www.ndsu.nodak.edu/entomology/topics/mimicry.htm

Review

Design an animal that is a secondary consumer and is adapted to survive in a habitat that has the following conditions:
- Hot during the day but cold at night
- Plenty of water available
- Trees close together shading the ground below
- Most of the prey animals live in the trees but they are easier to catch when they go down to the ground
- The tertiary consumers live on the ground.

Draw a diagram of your animal and label it to explain how it is adapted to these conditions.

Chapter summary

In this chapter you have found out that:
- Animals have adapted to their habitats in a variety of ways in order to survive.
- Camouflage is an adaptation to avoid being seen by predators or prey.
- Prey animals adapt to avoid being eaten and so predators must adapt so that they can continue to catch them.

Peppered moths

Introduction

In this chapter, we look at the classic study of the peppered moth population.

- The adaptations of some organisms allow them to live more successfully in some areas than in others.
- Habitats change over time, and the organisms that live there must adapt to these changes or their populations die out.
- The study of peppered moths demonstrates this adaptation to a changing environment.

Sc1 Put these stages of a scientific investigation into the correct sequence and join them with arrows to make a flow chart:

- Test the hypothesis
- Draw conclusions from the data
- Consider the present scientific evidence
- Evaluate the conclusion and compare with previous scientific evidence
- Use data already collected to help develop a hypothesis
- Analyse the data

Natural selection

For thousands of years, humans have *artificially selected* the characteristics of the offspring of plants and animals. They have done this by choosing which parents to breed together. By this process, humans have developed crops, farm animals and pets.

Many millions of years before humans arrived, in fact since organisms first came into existence, a process of *natural selection* has been taking place on Earth. The physical characteristics of the environment have determined which individuals live or die. Those that survive get to breed with each other and pass their own characteristics on to the next generation.

The first person to describe the process of natural selection was Charles Darwin in 1859. He used the idea to explain his Theory of Evolution that described how the organisms on the planet had evolved and changed gradually over time: those adapted to the environment survived, and the others died out and became extinct.

In 1960, Dr Kettlewell of Oxford University reported on his investigations into the populations of peppered moths. This was one of the first studies that demonstrated natural selection in action.

What Dr Kettlewell knew

Dr Kettlewell already knew that the peppered moth (species *Biston betularia*) came in two varieties. There was a pale variety with white wings and black spots, and a dark variety with completely black wings.

It was common in the nineteenth century for people to collect, preserve and mount moths for display. These records show that all the peppered moths used to be of the pale variety. Then in 1845, the first specimen of the black variety was caught in Manchester. At the time, there was some debate about whether or not it was definitely a peppered moth, but close examination showed that it was the same species as the pale variety.

By 1895, 98 per cent of the Manchester population of peppered moths were the black variety.

Dr Kettlewell was able to track down over one hundred years of data showing that the black variety of peppered moth was increasing, but only in the industrial areas of Britain and Europe.

1 Set up a light trap to collect the moths that live in your area. You will need:
- white sheet
- cardboard egg boxes
- bright torch
- moth identification key

This is what you do:

1 Hang up the white sheet between two trees in a suitable area

2 Place the egg boxes at the base

3 Position the torch to shine on to the white sheet

4 Leave overnight so that the moths will be attracted to the light and will crawl down the sheet into the egg boxes

5 Collect the boxes first thing next morning to identify the moths you have collected

6 Keep handling of the moths to a minimum as their wings are very delicate

7 Release the moths in the area they were collected

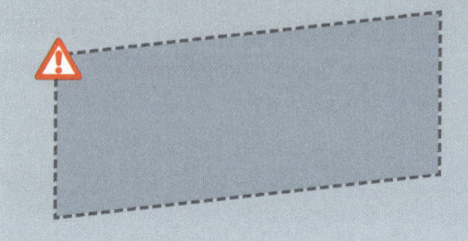

Dr Kettlewell's hypothesis

Dr Kettlewell used the data that he had collected to develop a hypothesis. His idea was that the black variety of peppered moth was being favoured by natural selection in the industrial areas. He said that this could be because the black wings would be better camouflaged against the tree trunks that had been blackened by soot.

Lichens, which survive in areas with clean air, mottle the bark of tree on which the pale form of the peppered moth is disguised. The black form is visible to predators.

In sooty areas, birds must have been eating many more of the pale moths than the black ones, because they stood out against the black of the trees. The black variety could then survive to breed and would pass on the black wing characteristic to the next generation of moths.

Gaining evidence

The historical evidence may have supported Dr Kettlewell's hypothesis, but to test whether it continued to apply, Dr Kettlewell needed more evidence.

Over the years, since the beginning of the industrial revolution in the eighteenth century, the trees had become blackened with soot. This meant that a particular characteristic of habitats with trees had changed. A change in the moth population, thought Dr Kettlewell, could be linked to this change in the environment. If he could collect *evidence* to show that this change had happened, then it would help to demonstrate an environmental influence that was driving natural selection. This would reinforce Darwin's Theory of Evolution.

In industrial areas where the air contains sulphur dioxide, no lichens can survive and tree bark is blackened by soot. But these conditions favour the black form of the peppered moth as it is well camouflaged.

Over the billions of years since life began on the planet, there must have been many millions of small changes in the environment. The populations of all living things would have been affected by these changes, and this helps to explain evolution.

A scientist, however, must collect data in a very precise way without looking for a particular answer. The data has to be analysed to describe what it shows before any conclusions can be drawn.

Testing the hypothesis

This is the method that Kettlewell used.

- He bred large numbers of both varieties of the peppered moth.
- In 1953, he took his moths to a polluted area of industrial Birmingham where the natural population of moths was made up of over 90% of the black variety.
- His moths were marked, so that they could be recognised again, and then released.
- Kettlewell also observed and filmed the feeding behaviour of birds. He saw robins, sparrows and redstarts feeding on the peppered moths.
- After a time, he set up a light trap to capture the moths. He looked for the mark he had put on them and so was able to count how many of the moths he caught had been released by him in the first place.
- In 1955, the mark/release/recapture method was repeated in a clean, unpolluted rural area of Dorset.

The results and the conclusions

1953 Birmingham peppered moths	Pale variety	Black variety
Numbers of moths marked and released	137	447
Numbers of moths recaptured	18	123

Kettlewell calculated the percentage of the pale variety of moths that he had recaptured:

$(18/137) \times 100 = 13\%$

1955 Dorset peppered moths	Pale variety	Black variety
Numbers of moths marked and released	496	473
Numbers of moths recaptured	62	30

Dr Kettlewell had also observed the birds actually feeding on the peppered moths. He had noticed that they were particularly quick at spotting the black variety when it landed on a tree that was clean and covered in lichens.

2 a Calculate the percentage of the black variety of moths that were recaptured in Birmingham in 1953.

b Copy and complete these sentences to conclude what this data tells you.

In the polluted area, a greater proportion of the _____ variety was recaptured. The _____ variety was therefore better camouflaged from the birds. The birds could see the _____ variety much more easily on the black trees, so feeding on them reduced their numbers. Only _____% of those released were recaptured compared to _____% of the black variety.

c Calculate the percentage of each variety recaptured in Dorset in 1955.

d Write your own conclusion explaining what this data tells you.

3 Discuss with a partner the possible reasons for the following techniques that Kettlewell used in his study:

a Mark/release/recapture

b Doing the observations and filming the birds feeding

c The two-year gap between the tests in the two different areas

d The fact that, for the moths released in 1955, the numbers of the two varieties were better balanced.

Why should we be interested in this study about moths? The reason is that studies like this can help us to understand the world we live in and how evolution and population changes occur. The studies also provide information that enables us to try to protect the natural world and its variety of organisms.

This study highlighted a number of important things:

- We can see evolution by natural selection happening in nature today.
- The soot from burning fossil fuels affected the trees and the organisms that lived on them.
- Governments around the world need to discuss the impact of industry on the natural world and the possible consequences of pollution.

The proportion of the black variety in the peppered moth population had increased, and this effect was given a name: industrial melanism. Industrial melanism has since been observed in many types of moth in Britain, elsewhere in Europe and in the USA.

4 Test the leaves from local trees to look at the pollution coating their surface. Ideally, leaves of the same variety should be tested so that direct comparisons can be made between pollution levels; holly leaves work well. You will need:
- collection of leaves from a number of trees of the same type
- sticky tape
- white paper

This is what you do:

1 Stick pieces of sticky tape onto the leaves

2 Rub the tape to lift off any material from the surface of the leaf

3 Stick the tape onto the paper and label each with the type of tree it came from, and its location

4 Compare the amount of grime lifted off the different leaves

Web Links
Visit these websites to find out more about peppered moths:
www.utm.edu/~rirwin/moth.htm
www.millerandlevine.com/km/evol/Moths/moths.html

Review
In 1956, the Clean Air Act was passed by the UK government and became law. Work with a partner to find out about this law, then explain the effect it should have on the populations of peppered moths around the country.

Chapter summary
In this chapter you have found out that:
- The characteristics of a population can be selected both naturally and artificially.
- Dr Kettlewell tested his hypothesis about natural selection in the peppered moth.
- Pollution can alter the environment and affect living organisms.
- Collecting data about changes in populations can help governments to determine whether pollution is harming the environment.

Lichens and air pollution

Introduction

In this chapter, we interpret the results of an investigation into the effect of air pollution on the growth of lichens.

- Lichens are a very special type of plant that have been successful all over the world for millions of years.
- Evidence suggests that lichens are sensitive to chemical pollution of the air.
- Scientists continue to collect data on lichen populations to indicate the levels of air pollution.

Sc1 Put the following stages of a scientific investigation into the correct order and join them with arrows.

- Present the data to look for patterns
- Plan safely how to collect accurate and reliable data
- Come to a conclusion
- Keep other variables constant for a fair test
- Describe the relationship between the independent and the dependent variable you are going to investigate
- Evaluate the results to see how reliable they are
- Analyse the data and describe the relationship it shows between the independent and dependent variables

The independent variable

In the study described below, the independent variable being investigated is *the effect of air pollution*.

Pollution of the air has increased since we began burning the fossil fuels coal, oil and gas. We burn them to release the energy that is stored chemically in these fuels. We use the energy to provide heat and to make electricity for transport and for the manufacture of goods.

Coal, oil and gas contain the chemical element sulphur. When sulphur burns, it joins with the oxygen in the air to make sulphur dioxide (SO_2).

sulphur + oxygen $\longrightarrow$ sulphur dioxide

Lichens are known to be particularly sensitive to SO_2 and other pollutant gases in the air.

The dependent variable

In this study, the dependent variable that will be measured is *the growth of lichens*.

Lichens are a very special type of plant. A lichen is actually two different organisms living together that form one plant body as they grow. Each type of lichen is composed of an alga living amongst the tissue of a fungus. Different lichens have different combinations of alga + fungus.

The lichen Xanthoria aureola is composed of a network of hyphae of the fungus, with the alga growing near the upper surface and giving the lichen its orange colour.

There are up to 20 000 species of lichens. Different lichens can survive practically anywhere in the world, from the poles to the desert. You are likely to find them on bare rocks, gravestones and tree bark. They grow slowly and survive on low levels of mineral nutrients. Some lichens in the Arctic may be 4500 years old.

Experiments in the 1970s found that some species of lichen could survive temperatures as low as −198 °C and that most lichens can carry out photosynthesis at −18.5 °C.

Colourful lichens

Litmus is an indicator that changes colour in acids and alkalis. The first litmus was made from lichens. Lichens are also the source of a wide range of dyes used to colour wool and other materials.

The relationship being investigated

Does air pollution affect the growth of lichens?

There is evidence to suggest that lichens can be completely killed by even low levels of air pollution.

The plan for the investigation

Scientists learnt that a new road was to be built next to a small wood a long way from any other roads. They thought that this would be the perfect opportunity to investigate whether pollution from the car exhausts would affect the lichens growing on the bark of the trees in the wood.

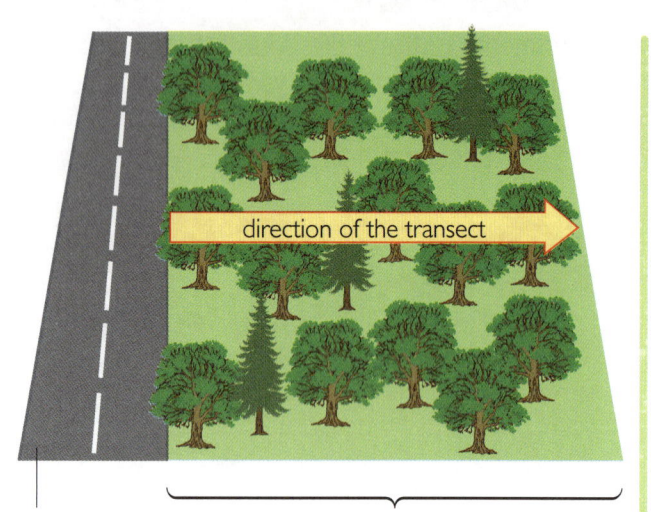

New road to be built here

woodland

direction of the transect

The scientists agreed to collect data from a line of trees that stretched through the woodland away from the planned road. This line is called a transect through the woodland. The tree trunks had lichens growing on them. The scientists decided to measure and record the percentage of lichen cover on an agreed section of trees, at regular intervals of 10 metres away from the road.

The aim was to take the measurements before the road was built and then to continue measuring for a number of years afterwards, to see if there was any effect on the growth of the lichens.

The data collected

The table shows the results before the road was built.

Distance from where the road will be (m)	Percentage of tree surface surveyed that was covered with lichens
1	68
11	74
21	75
31	65
41	81
51	80
61	78
71	76
81	66
91	73

1 Draw a line graph of these results. Put the distance from the road along the horizontal axis and the percentage cover by lichens on the vertical axis.

2 Describe the relationship shown on the graph by copying and completing the following sentence:

The graph shows that as the distance from where the road will be built increases, the percentage of lichens …

3 Give a reason why you think the scientists took measurements before the road was even built.

Results were also collected for some years after the road was built.

Year	Percentage cover by lichens at each distance from the road										Comment
	1 m	11 m	21 m	31 m	41 m	51 m	61 m	71 m	81 m	91 m	
Road built	15	24	28	29	33	36	35	34	31	38	Biggest decrease in numbers
1 year later	15	23	27	29	33	37	37	37	32	40	Little time to recover
2 years later	15	24	28	29	34	39	39	40	35	44	Small amount of recovery further from the road
5 years later	16	26	31	33	39	45	46	48	44	54	Increasing recovery, greater further from the road

4 Plot the results for each of the years onto the same axes you used in Activity 1. Give each year its own colour, or label it so that you can recognise which line represents each year.

5 a Describe what happened to the population of lichens growing in the woodland in the year that the road was built.

b Explain what might have caused this change in the lichen population.

6 Describe what happened to the population of lichens 1 year later. Explain the difference in the results compared to the year the road was built.

7 Use the figures for 2 and 5 years later to describe how quickly the lichens were able to recover.

8 Choose the results from the table that the scientists used to come to this conclusion.

9 The results 5 years after the road was built showed that the lichens were starting to recover. Give reasons to explain why this might be.

10 Is it possible to predict the percentage cover of lichens 10 years after the road was built? Give reasons to explain your answer.

11 Describe further evidence the scientists could collect to make their results more reliable.

Conclusion

- The results of the investigation show that building a road did lead to a decrease in the numbers of lichens growing in nearby woodland.
- In the year the road was built, mechanical equipment and works traffic would have released gases that polluted the air. This air pollution would be at its highest level next to the road, but would decrease further away.
- The scientists concluded that:

Air pollution does affect the growth of lichens.

Why are lichens important?

Lichens are important to us, to the environment and as organisms on the planet:

- They are useful indicators of pollution. (For our own survival we should minimise pollution in the air that we breathe.) The numbers of lichens decrease when air pollution increases by even a small amount, so we can use the numbers to indicate how much pollution there is in the air.

- They are important in the environment as they help to erode rocks and break them down into soil. Soil is needed to grow other types of plant.

- Lichens take a long time to grow (between 1 mm and 1 cm each year), and high levels of air pollution could cause them to become extinct. This would reduce the diversity of life on Earth.

Review

Write a letter to the Government Department of Transport to explain:
- The type of pollution caused by the building of roads and the traffic that uses them
- The effects of this pollution
- What can be done to reduce the pollution.

Chapter summary

In this chapter you have found out that:
- Data from the environment can be collected scientifically to look for relationships between variables.
- Scientists have gathered evidence to show that when the level of pollution in the air increases, the number of lichen types decreases.
- We can use the growth of lichens to indicate the level of air pollution.

Extinctions

Introduction

In this chapter, we consider what happens to the organisms that do not adapt successfully to the changes in their habitat.

- Life has been reacting to changes on this planet for 3000 million years.
- Extinction is when all the individuals of a particular species die out.
- The extinction of one species will affect all the others in the food web.
- Man is bringing about rapid changes in the environment that are causing much extinction around the world.

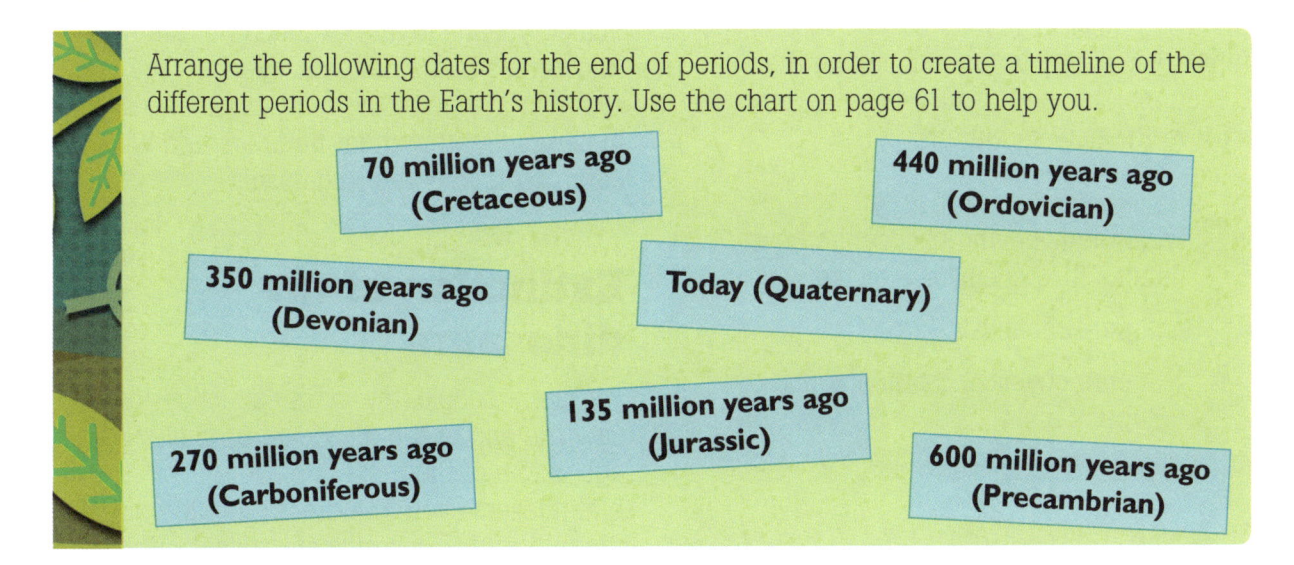

Arrange the following dates for the end of periods, in order to create a timeline of the different periods in the Earth's history. Use the chart on page 61 to help you.

- 70 million years ago (Cretaceous)
- 440 million years ago (Ordovician)
- 350 million years ago (Devonian)
- Today (Quaternary)
- 270 million years ago (Carboniferous)
- 135 million years ago (Jurassic)
- 600 million years ago (Precambrian)

Since life began

Scientists believe that the Earth itself was formed about 4500 million years ago. For the next 1000 million years, chemical elements were reacting with each other to form molecules. One of these was DNA, a special molecule because it is capable of making copies of itself. 3400 million years ago, a protective coat developed around the DNA, forming the first living things – bacteria.

Organisms all over the world evolved from these simple bacteria. It wasn't until 3 million years ago, however, that humans first appeared.

This evolution had been brought about by the constant changes in the environment. Some of these changes were gradual; some organisms would adapt to them and continue to survive, but others would become extinct. Extinction of a species happens when the number being born does not replace the number dying. The number of individuals in the population begins to decrease until there are no more left. How long this process takes depends on how big the change in the environment is.

Some changes are sudden, so that organisms have very little time to adapt. We know, from the evidence that we have found, that these sudden changes can lead to mass extinctions.

A mass extinction is when many different species disappear, leaving no offspring to pass their genes on to the next generation.

Extinctions are a fact of life on this planet. If the dinosaurs had not become extinct when they did, mammals might not have evolved into the dominant life form on the planet. At the time of the dinosaurs, most of the mammals that existed were small rodent-like animals. A great deal more, including ourselves, have developed since then.

Having knowledge about how extinctions happen can help us to adapt to the changes that the human race may have to face in the future. It will require us to maintain the conditions we need to survive, or to adapt to survive the new conditions.

> **5** Visit this website to see what mammals were like at the time of the dinosaurs:
> www.bbc.co.uk/beasts/evidence/prog1/page5.shtml

Ice ages and mass extinctions

Since the first invertebrates appeared, there have been at least three major ice ages. They have occurred about 150 million years apart and each one has lasted between 10 and 50 million years.

Global ice ages have been linked with mass extinctions. For example, approximately 300 million years ago, the extinction of the Ammonites had a dramatic effect on the rest of the food web in the sea. Ammonites were molluscs found in great numbers and were eaten by many other organisms.

Extinction of the dinosaurs

For many people, the mass extinction that saw the end of the dinosaurs 65 million years ago is one of the most interesting brainteasers ever! The dinosaurs died out at the end of the Mesozoic era, along with the ichthyosaurs, plesiosaurs, pterosaurs, and many invertebrate groups.

> **1** From the following choose the best definition of 'chemical element':
> - **a** a pure chemical
> - **b** a pure chemical containing just one type of atom
> - **c** a chemical that contains just one atom
>
> **2** Look up the full name of the chemical DNA.
>
> **3** Calculate the number of years between the arrival of bacteria and the arrival of humans.
>
> **4 a** List the sorts of gradual changes in the environment that organisms would need to adapt to. Compare your list with a partner.
> **b** Work with your partner to make a list of sudden changes in the environment that could lead to mass extinctions.

The development of life during the history of the Earth

Millions of years ago	Era	Period	Examples of organisms	Ice ages
0	Cenozoic	Quaternary	Humans dominant	Cenozoic
50	Cenozoic	Tertiary	Mammals become dominant	
100	Mesozoic	Cretaceous	Flowering plants first appeared Birds first appeared	
150	Mesozoic	Jurassic	Conifers grew Dinosaurs flourished	
200	Mesozoic	Triassic	Reptiles flourished	
250	Palaeozoic	Permian		Permo-Carboniferous
300	Palaeozoic	Carboniferous	Coal formed	
350	Palaeozoic	Devonian	Amphibians first appeared	
400	Palaeozoic	Silurian	Fish first appeared	
450	Palaeozoic	Ordovician	Giant horsetails grew Invertebrates first appeared on land	Late Ordovician
500	Palaeozoic	Cambrian	Tree ferns grew Marine invertebrates, especially trilobites, flourished	
600		Precambrian	Single-celled organisms, e.g. bacteria, flourished	Varangian

Ichthyosaur, a marine reptile that became extinct by the end of the Mesozoic era.

People from all over the world have tried to provide theories to explain what actually caused this mass extinction. Here are just a few of those theories.

Theory	Effects	Evidence
The Earth was hit by an asteroid at least 10 km wide.	Dust containing iridium (a chemical element found in large amounts in rocks from outer space) is released into the air; dust blocks out the sunlight for one or two years and the food chain breaks down; acidic gases are released and lead to acid rain.	Rocks that formed at the end of the Mesozoic contain high levels of iridium.
The Earth was hit by a shower of comets.		
Many volcanic eruptions occurred around the world.	Dust blocks out the sunlight for one or two years and the food chain breaks down; release of acidic gases lead to acid rain.	
The dinosaurs became too big and ran out of food.	The producers at the start of the food chain could not provide enough energy to support such large animals.	
Herbivore dinosaurs were poisoned by plants.	Herbivore dinosaurs starve, so there are fewer for the carnivore dinosaurs to eat.	Plants developed the use of poisons at this time.
Caterpillars competed with the herbivore dinosaurs for the leaves.		

6 Calculate the number of years in between the extinction of the dinosaurs and the appearance of man.

7 In a group, discuss the different theories shown in the table and decide the answers to the following questions.

   a How did the scientists calculate the size of the asteroid?

   b What further evidence might scientists collect to help prove any of the theories?

   c What is the difference between an asteroid and a comet?

   d Name the process that plants cannot carry out if the sunlight is blocked by dust.

   e Name one of the acidic gases that can cause acid rain.

   f Why would it be useful for plants to evolve the use of poisons?

   g Which theory seems to you the most likely cause of the dinosaur extinction? Give reasons for your choice.

Extinction of the dodo

The dodo was a species of bird that lived about 300 years ago on the island of Mauritius. The disappearance of the dodo is famous because it is one of the first reported extinctions caused by humans.

People hunted the dodo until there were no more left.

Reporting extinctions

The following news items were reported in *The Guardian* in May 2003.

Fall in fish stocks hits crisis point

The world's great marine predators are being wiped out. Populations of marlin, swordfish, tuna and rays have crashed by more than 90% since the advent of industrial scale fishing, according to research published today ...

... What worries many scientists is that the oceans' big fish are being wiped out despite restrictions on how intensively they are fished. The restrictions are hard to enforce and easy to abuse.

Bans and quotas are only effective if the fish can reproduce fast enough to replace those that are fished out or die in other ways. 'The answer is to turn back the clock to a time when there were still plenty of areas that were off limits to fishing,' said Prof Roberts (professor of marine ecology at the University of York). That means the creation of 'national parks in the sea'.

Ian Sample, Science Correspondent

EXTINCTION STARES 25 SPECIES IN THE FACE

In the nineteenth century, there were around 15 species of tortoise in the Galapagos Islands. Over the past 100 years, four have been hunted to extinction and the remaining 11 are critically endangered. Next to step into oblivion will be the Abingdon island tortoise. When 60-year-old George dies in about a century, that will be it for a creature that outlived the dinosaurs.

All around the world, tortoises and freshwater turtles are in crisis. Of the 300 species alive today, experts agree that 200 are under serious threat. A list published by the Turtle Conservation Fund (TCF) focuses on 25 species which they say will become extinct within the next two decades unless immediate action is taken.

Alok Jha, Science Correspondent

Modern-day extinctions

Humans were causing extinctions before they realised the serious impact this could have on the environment. In the 1950s, zoos were still taking animals from the wild believing there to be an unlimited supply. Nowadays, the movement of animals is in the opposite direction: practically every zoo in the world has at least one captive breeding programme, breeding animals that are close to extinction and then returning them to the wild.

Unfortunately, the speed of destruction of the world's natural habitats means that these animals have fewer and fewer places to live.

Also, as humans have spread across the globe, they have caused extinctions by introducing foreign species of animals to areas where they would not normally live. These have fed on local animals and plants, wiping out their populations.

Bird found – then habitat destroyed

It is a story that sums up the struggles facing conservationists. A new finch-like bird is identified for the first time in eastern Venezuela, and within two years its habitat has been destroyed to make way for a hydroelectric dam.

New Scientist, 1 November 2003

Scientists have estimated that by the year 2025 one-third of all the species of animal in the world will be threatened by extinction. We can only hypothesise about the effects this might have on the survival of our own species.

8 Look in an atlas to find the areas of the world that are mentioned in this chapter. The places to find are: Mauritius, Venezuela, and the Galapagos Islands.

9 Why should we worry about the decrease in the numbers of fish? List as many reasons as you can think of, and compare your list with a partner.

10 With your partner, list the types of 'immediate action' that might help to save the 25 species of tortoise and turtle from extinction.

Web Links

Visit these websites to find out more about extinction:

www.ucmp.berkeley.edu/diapsids/extinction.html

www.bbc.co.uk/dinosaurs/

www.bbc.co.uk/education/darwin/exfiles/index.htm

Review

Below is a list of changes that could happen in the world today. Work in a group to choose one issue from the list, and decide the effect it could have on the human population if it happened now:

- Increased sunlight
- Ice age
- Many of the fish we eat becoming extinct
- All the rainforests around the world chopped down

Chapter summary

In this chapter you have found out that:

- The physical environment has been constantly changing since the Earth was formed about 4500 million years ago.
- Some species of organisms have successfully adapted to these changes, while others have become extinct.
- Mass extinctions are caused by sudden or extreme changes in the environment.

Fish farming

Introduction

In this chapter, we look at how and why fish are being farmed.

- Over-fishing has reduced the populations of fish in the sea.
- People have farmed animals for thousands of years.
- Fish are farmed to increase production of food.
- Fish farming can cause problems in the environment.

As a class, make a list on the board of all the different types of fish you have eaten. Discuss what this list tells you about fish in our diet.

Were there any surprises? Was it a long list?

Over-fishing

For many years, cod has been the favourite fish eaten by the people of Britain. The demand for cod around the world has led to a dramatic decrease in the numbers of cod swimming in the seas. This fall in numbers means that we describe cod as being over-fished.

When humans began to eat fish, they became the top predator of a food chain in the sea:

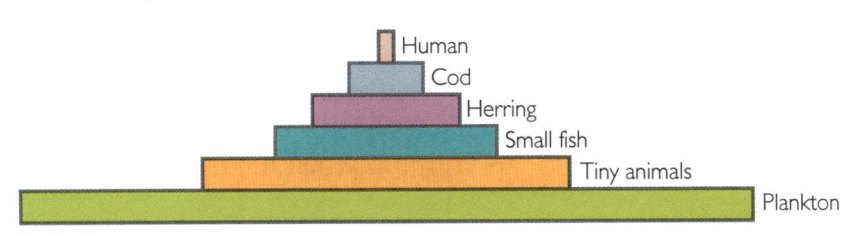

Plankton → Tiny animals → Small fish → Herring → Cod → Human

Whenever there is a change in a food chain, the numbers of all the other organisms will be affected. A dramatic increase in the size of the human population has led to over-fishing which has affected the entire food chain.

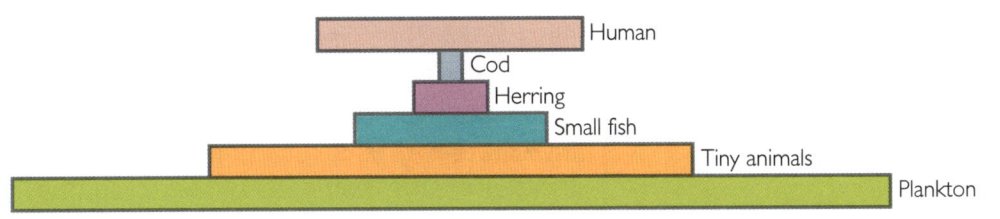

There is a risk that we could take so many fish from the seas that some species actually become extinct.

> **1 a** Which organisms in the food chain are the producers?
>
> **b** What can the producers do that the other organisms cannot?
>
> **2** Work with a partner to list as many reasons as you can for the increase in the human population. Compare your list with another group.
>
> **3** Choose which of the following best describes what happens when a species becomes extinct:
>
> **a** The number being born
>   = the number that die
>
> **b** The number being born
>   > the number that die
>
> **c** The number being born
>   < the number that die

Farming fish

Humans have been farming animals for thousands of years. We have done this so that we can control and create the food that we need to stay alive.

Fish farming is a way to increase the number of fish we have available to eat.

Salmon

Salmon was one of the first types of fish to be farmed. Young salmon are kept in tanks of fresh water and the food that they eat is controlled. They are then moved into cages, which are put in the sea. There can be between 5000 and 50 000 fish in each cage.

Today, every year, over 1 million tonnes of salmon come from fish farms worldwide.

Salmon

Trout

Cod

Halibut

Trout

Britain alone produces 35 million trout each year in fish farms. The trout are bred very carefully to increase the number of female fish, since people agree that female trout taste better than the male trout.

Cod

Cod are mainly farmed in Norway. When fish are farmed, more fish survive to become adult than they do in the wild. Farms can supply us with cod when the numbers in the sea are very low.

Halibut

Farming halibut has only started quite recently. Again, Norway is leading the way with this new farming technique.

Since 1984, the sales of fish from farms all around the world has increased by 11%. No other supply of food has increased this fast. In 2001, it was estimated that 29% of all the fish that were eaten in the world came from farms. Today, you can check whether or not you are eating farmed fish, as it must be written on the label of the food packet.

The fish farming industry has been estimated to be worth $54 billion!

> **4** Work with a partner to list as many farm animals as you can think of. Compare your list with another group.
>
> **5 a** Use a dictionary to find out how many kilograms are in one tonne.
>
> **b** Use an atlas to find the position of Norway.
>
> **6** As a class, brainstorm all the reasons why a larger number of fish survive in a fish farm than they do in the wild.
>
> **7** Draw a pie chart to represent the percentage of all the fish that came from farms in 2001, and the number that were caught from the sea.
>
> **8** Visit this website to find out more about fish farming:
> **www.fishfarming.co.uk**

The problems of farming fish

To farm fish for food, we need a place for the fish to breed and live, food to give them and ways to keep them fit and healthy.

In the process of working out the best ways to farm each fish type, fish farmers have had problems providing all these things correctly. Sometimes the fish are overcrowded, which means that they compete with each other for oxygen in the water. Trout have been observed in fish farms gasping for air at the water's surface.

The fish are usually fed on 'trash fish' which are the fish caught from the sea that we do not eat ourselves. It has been calculated that to grow a tonne of cod in a fish farm, you need to feed them 5 tonnes of 'trash fish'. Some people see this as a waste of the resources from the sea, and there is, of course, the risk of passing on diseases from the wild to the farmed fish.

Chemicals are used to reduce the chance of the farmed fish catching diseases. These chemicals are then passed up the food chain to us when we eat the fish.

The waste that the farmed fish produce can also pollute the environment.

Genetically modified farm fish

An American company has genetically modified salmon to produce a variety that can grow five times faster than wild salmon, but they eat less food. The aim is to increase the numbers of farmed salmon, so that we will be guaranteed salmon as a source of food.

The concern is that these GM fish might escape and wipe out the wild salmon. The GM fish might eat the wild salmon, or breed with them to produce new varieties of salmon that are not adapted to survive.

The US National Academy of Sciences is studying the new GM salmon to try and answer these questions.

Improving fish farming

Fish are an important part of our diet, so it is important that we help them to survive. It is also important that the fish we eat are healthy, nutritious and free from pollution and disease.

Fish farmers are learning better ways to run their farms. The use of chemicals to keep the fish healthy is controlled and the conditions that the fish are kept in are improving.

Some cod farmers have changed what they feed to their fish. They actually recreate the natural food chain at their farm. Algae are grown in large tanks and then fed to shrimps, which are kept in another tank. The shrimps can then be given to the cod in the fish farm as live food.

Algae ➡ Shrimp ➡ Cod ➡ Human

This seems more natural than feeding the fish on ground-up 'trash fish'.

Fish farming is set to increase over the coming years. This will be necessary if we want to keep eating the amount of fish we have been in the past. Without the fish farms, there just won't be enough fish in the sea to feed the human population.

9 How are fish adapted to breathe in water?

10 To reduce disease, fish are vaccinated and given antibiotics. One of these prevents disease and the other cures disease. Which is which?

11 Draw a pyramid of numbers to represent the numbers in the cod and shrimp food chain shown on the left.

Review

Look at each of the following statements and decide whether or not you agree with each one.

Fish should not be kept in crowded tanks when they are normally free to swim in the sea.

We should be spending money on protecting fish in the wild rather than on fish farms.

Fish farms will protect fish from going extinct.

Chapter summary

In this chapter you have found out that:
- Humans have over-fished the seas as the human population has increased.
- Over-fishing affects food webs in the sea.
- Fish are being farmed to increase their numbers so that we can continue to eat them in the future.
- Fish farming needs to be safe for the fish, for humans and for the environment.

GM crops

Introduction

In this chapter, we debate the reasons for and against genetically modified crops.

- Crops are plants that we grow for food.
- Crops are the producers in our food web.
- Crops can be genetically modified to increase the amount of food they produce.
- Maximising how much food we produce can affect other plants and animals.

GM crops are crops that have been genetically modified. This means that a gene controlling one particular characteristic has been copied from one living thing and then put into another living thing, in this case a crop plant. This crop will then develop with the desired characteristic that the copied gene controls.

There are many possible benefits from creating plants with particular useful characteristics, but there could be disadvantages too.

Decide which side of the table you are going to sit on at the beginning of the debate on GM crops.

For

Against

The debate

Follow the discussion group's arguments on this page and the next. Think carefully about each point that they make, and decide what your own opinion is.

For   **Against**

- Genes can be put into crops to make them harmful to insect pests and resistant to diseases.

- If insect pests are destroyed, the rest of the food web will be affected.
- The insect pests might move on to feed on other plants that are just as important as the crops.
- These mutant crops might affect the decomposers in the soil. The worms, bacteria and fungi might not be able to break them down and return the minerals to the soil. Farmers would then have to use more fertiliser to replace the minerals.

69

- GM crops would reduce the need to add chemicals to the soil. If they are naturally protected against pests and diseases, we won't need to spray them with chemicals like pesticides.

- What happens if the GM crops breed with other plants? Pollen from the crop plants might pollinate the weeds. The weeds might pick up the characteristics of the crop and become resistant to weed-killer. How would we get rid of the weeds then? How would we stop them growing out of control and competing with our crops for space, light, water and minerals in the soil? We might have to return to the days when we had to dig weeds out by hand.

- One concern is that GM crops might cause a large number of extinctions. We have no idea of the long-term effects such changes might have on the natural environment.

- We need to concentrate on helping our own species to survive. GM crops can be made more nutritional and healthy for us to eat. We can get them to grow faster and bigger than ever before. We can also get plants to grow in conditions that normally would not be suitable, such as during a drought, a flood or when it is really cold. There are 100 million people in the world that are starving, mainly because they live in areas where it is difficult to grow crops. Another 800 million around the world are hungry and, with the human population still increasing, we need to find ways of feeding everybody.

- Feeding the world is a very strong argument for GM crops. If it does go ahead, then it should be for this reason. However, should we risk experimenting with the unknown? This is a new technology and we know little about the long-term effects. Is it safe to tamper with the very producers of our own food chain?

- Scientists have been testing GM crops for years. They begin with two years of tests in the lab. The new GM crop is produced and then they breed them over many generations. All of the characteristics of the offspring are checked. Scientists look to see that the crop does have the characteristic that is wanted without any harmful effects.

- If the tests in the lab shows the crop to be safe, the scientists then move on to field trials. Farmers apply to test out the new GM crops in their fields. They must follow lots of rules and regulations if they are to be given permission by the government and their scientists. The trial is watched closely by the scientists to check that there is no harm to the environment.

- All this time, effort and money could be better spent on organic farming – the food tastes better, is better for us and it is better for the environment.

1 Work with a partner who has chosen to sit on the opposite side of the table to you, and list the types of crops we grow around the world. Compare your list with another group.

2 Work with your partner to list insects that are the pests of our crops because they eat them or damage them. Compare your list with another group.

3 a Which part of a plant absorbs the minerals from the soil to help it grow?

  b Why are plants called the producers of a food chain?

4 Decide which of the following is the best description of organic farming:

  a Farming in small fields

  b Having a mixture of animals on the farm

  c Growing crops without the use of chemicals

  d Not using machinery in the fields

5 Look carefully at each of the comments made in the debate. Choose one and write down a reply that you would have made to this comment.

6 Work in a group of four to discuss the comments you have written down. Take it in turn to read out comments, leaving time for anyone to respond.

Web Links

Visit these websites to find out more about GM crops:

www.csa.com/hottopics/gmfood/overview
www.pbs.org/wgbh/harvest/
www.foodfuture.org.uk/

Review

After hearing the arguments for and against GM crops, make a final decision about which side of the table you would sit on. Write an explanation of why you have chosen to sit there.

Chapter summary

In this chapter you have found out that:
- Scientists are experimenting with our crops by modifying the genes to give plants particular characteristics.
- There are huge benefits to this, as we could grow healthier crops on a larger scale without the use of chemical pesticides.
- There are risks to consider, since we could affect the delicate balance of the food webs around the world, which could lead to extinctions.

Pesticides versus biological control

Introduction

In this chapter, we look at two different ways of controlling pests.

- Humans grow crops as a source of food.
- Other animals feed on and damage our crops.
- These animals are called pests.
- Pesticides or biological control can be used to kill the pests.

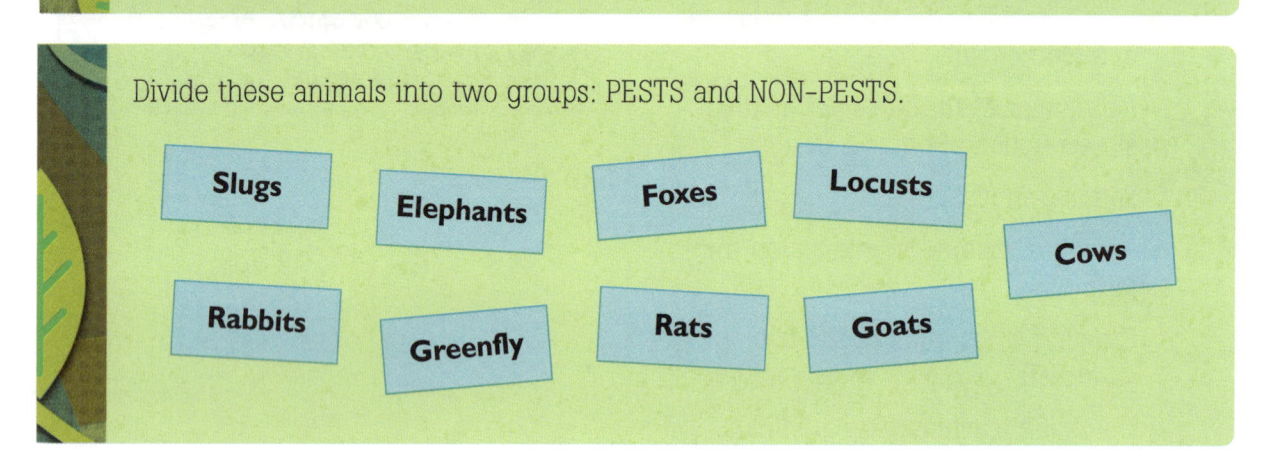

Divide these animals into two groups: PESTS and NON-PESTS.

- Slugs
- Elephants
- Foxes
- Locusts
- Cows
- Rabbits
- Greenfly
- Rats
- Goats

Controlling pests

Pest animals can destroy our crops or make them unfit for us to eat. The amount of a crop we harvest is called the yield. To increase the yield we have to decrease the number of pests. There are two major ways of doing this.

Pesticides

Pesticides are chemicals that kill pests. For example, fruit trees can be sprayed to kill the insects feeding on them.

Biological control

Natural predators of a pest can be used to control its numbers. The predators eat the pests and keep their numbers down. If the number of predators is increased, the number of pests will decrease even more. For example, extra ladybirds can be released to control the number of greenfly.

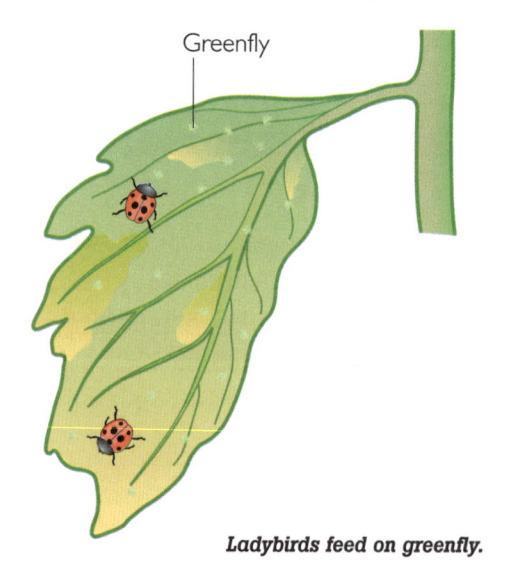

Ladybirds feed on greenfly.

Advantages and disadvantages

Different pests need to be controlled in different ways, and farmers need to look at the advantages and disadvantages of each method before deciding which one to use.

Pesticides		Biological control	
Advantages	**Disadvantages**	**Advantages**	**Disadvantages**
Quick and easy to use. Effective. Farmer can control which crops will be sprayed.	Chemicals can be washed off when it rains. Pesticides might build up in the food chain and poison non-pest animals, including humans.	The predators are found naturally in the environment. A predator can be chosen that only feeds on the pest. When the pests die out, so do the predators.	It takes time to breed and release the predators. The predators cannot be controlled once they have been released. If the predators increase in number, they may harm the environment.

It seems then that there are a number of reasons for and against each method.

> **1** Work in a group of four. Each of you should take responsibility for one of the sections of the table above.
>
> You have 10 minutes to prepare a speech that you will give to a farmer (your teacher!). You have to persuade the farmer that your argument is the most important thing they have to consider when it comes to reducing the number of pests.

Investigating pest control

A farmer decides to test the two methods of controlling pests. She grows tomatoes in three greenhouses and decides to use these to investigate the effect of the methods on the yield of tomatoes.

> **2 a** What is the independent variable being investigated?
>
> **b** What is the dependent variable being measured?

Control   Pesticide   Biological control

The farmer decides to leave one of the greenhouses as a control. No method of pest control will be used in this greenhouse. The tomatoes in the second greenhouse will be treated with pesticide to kill greenfly. Ladybirds will be released in the third greenhouse as a form of biological control; the ladybirds are predators of the greenfly.

3 What is the reason for setting up a control experiment?

The farmer then chooses a suitable sample size. 500 tomato plants will be grown in each greenhouse and the yield of tomatoes they produce will be measured by weighing them.

4 Complete this sentence to demonstrate what you understand about the importance of sample size:

The larger the sample size, the more _____ the results.

Several variables have to be kept constant for a fair test. The farmer lists all the things that she thinks she will need to keep the same:

- Variety of tomato
- Age of the tomato plants
- Type of compost the plants grow in
- Mass of compost the plants grow in
- Volume of water given to the plants
- Time when the plants are watered
- Temperature of the greenhouses
- Amount of sunlight reaching the plants

5 Copy and complete the table below.

6 Mass, volume, time, temperature and amount of sunlight all need to be measured to make sure they are kept constant. For each, name the apparatus that could be used to measure them and give the units of measurement.

7 List any other variables that will need to be kept constant for a fair test that the farmer hasn't thought about.

Web Links

Visit these websites to find out more about pest control:

www.foodstandards.gov.uk/safereating/pesticides/
www.pesticides.gov.uk/
www.defenders.co.uk/

Fair test point	Why it needs to be kept constant	Possible effect on the results if not kept constant
Tomato variety	Different varieties grow at different rates to a range of different sizes.	The yield will depend on the variety as well as on the method of pest control.
Age of tomato plants		
Type of compost used	Different types contain different amounts of minerals.	
Mass of compost		
Volume of water	Water is needed for photosynthesis. The volume of water will affect how quickly the plants can make glucose.	
Time when the plants are watered		
Greenhouse temperature	Temperature affects how quickly a plant can carry out photosynthesis.	
Amount of sunlight		Plants with more light can carry out more photosynthesis. They will grow faster and this will increase the yield of tomatoes.

Review

Work with a partner to use what you have learnt about the use of pesticides and biological control to predict the results of the farmer's investigation. Which greenhouse do you think will create the greatest yield of tomatoes, and which the least? Give reasons to explain your prediction.

Chapter summary

In this chapter you have found out that:
- Pesticides are chemicals that kill the pests of our crops.
- Biological control uses the predators of the pests to reduce their numbers.
- There are advantages and disadvantages to each method of pest control.
- Fair tests need to be carried out to investigate the effectiveness of each method.

Global warming and flooding

Introduction

In this chapter, we learn about global warming and its effects on our environment.

- The greenhouse effect makes this planet suitable for life.
- Human activity is increasing the levels of greenhouse gases in the atmosphere.
- The temperature of the Earth is increasing.
- Physical changes affect life on the planet.

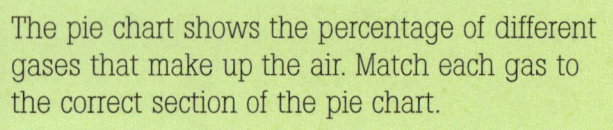

The pie chart shows the percentage of different gases that make up the air. Match each gas to the correct section of the pie chart.

Carbon dioxide

Nitrogen

Other gases

Oxygen

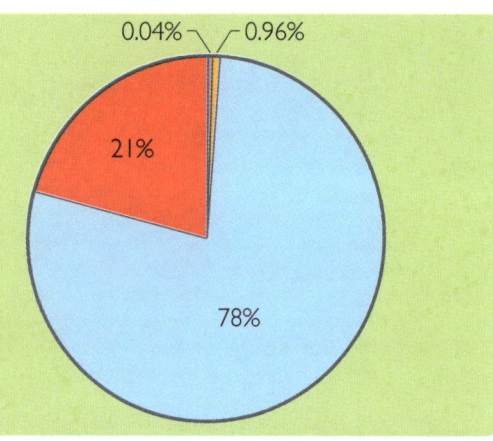

The greenhouse effect

A layer of gases, called the atmosphere, surrounds planet Earth. The atmosphere makes this planet suitable for life. This is because of the greenhouse effect.

Carbon dioxide, methane, and nitrogen oxides are examples of greenhouse gases in our atmosphere. They behave like the glass in a greenhouse. Light energy from the Sun passes through our atmosphere and warms up the land and the sea. Heat from the Earth's surface then travels back up through the atmosphere. Some of the heat escapes into space, but the greenhouse gases reflect a lot of the heat back down to Earth, in the way that glass reflects heat back inside a greenhouse.

The heat that is reflected back keeps the Earth warm and gives us a temperature that is suitable for life. The average temperature of the Earth is approximately 22 °C; in some areas it drops to −20 °C and in others it increases to 40 °C.

We can compare these temperatures to the Moon that has no atmosphere and, therefore, no greenhouse effect. On the Moon the temperature can drop to −150 °C and increase to 150 °C. This means it is either too hot or too cold for life.

Without the greenhouse effect we would not be able to survive on this planet.

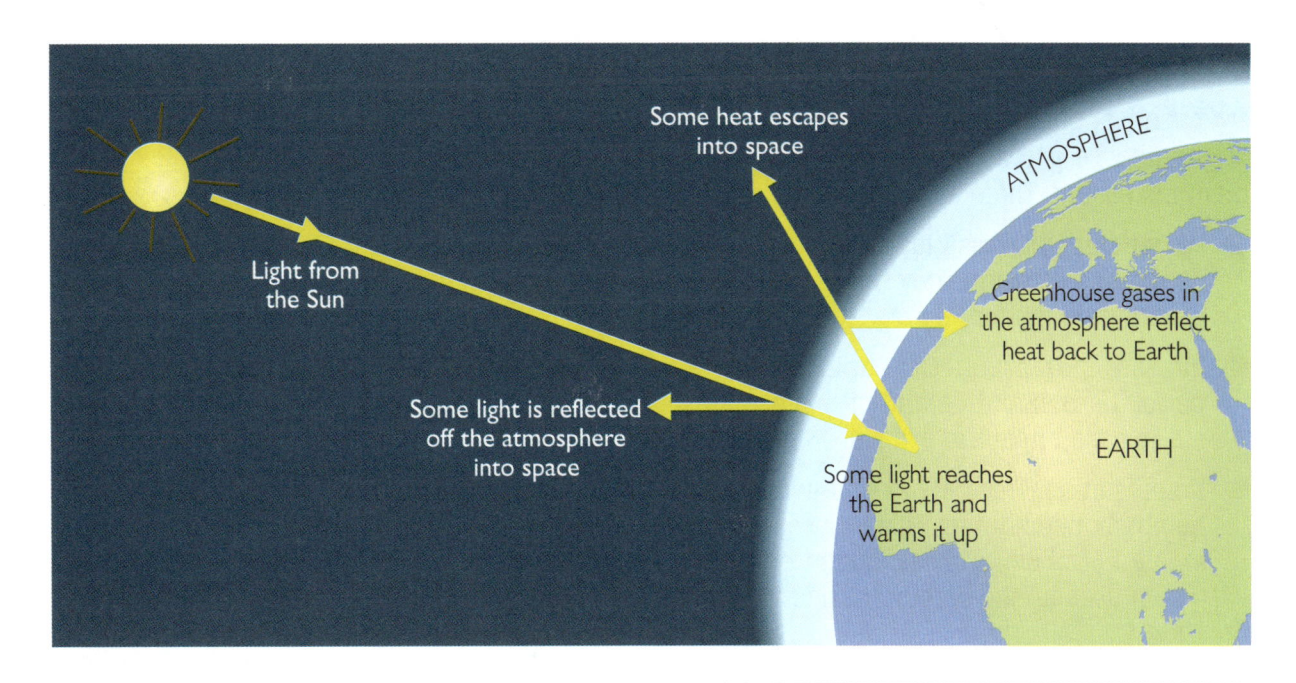

Diagram: Light from the Sun travels to Earth. Some light is reflected off the atmosphere into space. Some light reaches the Earth and warms it up. Some heat escapes into space. Greenhouse gases in the atmosphere reflect heat back to Earth. Labels: ATMOSPHERE, EARTH.

1 Complete the word equation to show the chemical reaction that produces carbon dioxide:

carbon + _____ ⟶ carbon dioxide

2 The range of temperatures on the Earth is from −20 to 40 °C; a difference of 60 °C. Calculate the difference in the range of temperatures on the Moon.

3 Investigate how effective gases are at keeping in the heat.

You will need:
- 2 conical flasks
- bubble wrap
- kettle
- 2 temperature probes connected to a data logger

⚠ Take care with boiling water.

This is what you do:

1 Set up the temperature probes and data logger to measure the temperature over 20 minutes

2 Boil the kettle and pour an equal volume of water into each conical flask

3 Wrap one of the flasks in bubble wrap and leave the other as a control

4 Insert the temperature probes and measure the decrease in temperature of the water over 20 minutes

5 Print out a line graph of the results to look for patterns in the data

4 Interpret the results from your investigation by answering the following questions:

a Why was an equal volume of water measured into each conical flask?

b Why was one of the flasks set up as a control?

c Why does the temperature of the water decrease in both conical flasks?

d Explain how the shape of the graph shows this decrease in temperature.

e Explain the difference in the shapes of the line graphs for each of the conical flasks.

f The bubble wrap has the gases of the air trapped in the bubbles. How does this affect the loss of heat from the conical flask?

Global warming

Over the last one hundred years, the amount of greenhouse gases in the atmosphere has been increasing. There are several causes:

- Power stations. Fossil fuels are burnt to generate electricity. They release carbon dioxide into the air.
- Increase in transport. Car engines burn petrol. Carbon dioxide and nitrogen oxides are released from the exhaust.
- Deforestation. Trees around the world are being chopped down. This reduces the amount of photosynthesis taking place, which uses up the carbon dioxide in the air.

Increasing the greenhouse gases is like making the glass in the greenhouse thicker. More heat energy is reflected back to Earth and the temperature of the world goes up. This increase in temperature is called global warming.

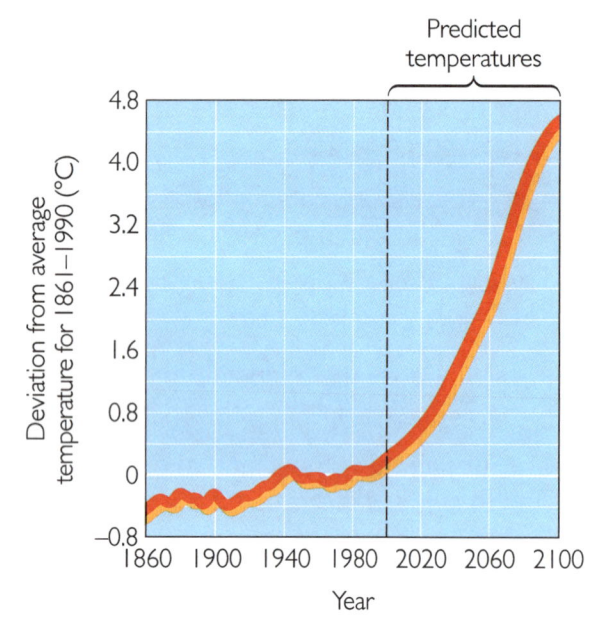

Average world temperature recorded from 1860 to the present, and as predicted to 2100.

5 Name two examples of fossil fuels.

6 Complete the word equation for photosynthesis:

$$\text{carbon dioxide} + \underline{\qquad} \xrightarrow[\text{chlorophyll}]{\text{sunlight}} \text{glucose} + \underline{\qquad}$$

The effects of global warming

We cannot be certain of the effect that the increase in the world's temperature will have – we can only make predictions. Scientists are concerned that the ice at the North and South Poles will melt. The extra water will make the sea levels rise and that will cause flooding at the coasts. Some areas of land may even be completely covered in water.

The temperature and the water levels will also affect the weather. It is likely that certain areas of the world will experience more floods or more droughts and this might make it difficult for us to grow crops.

Report from the Environment Agency

The job of the Environment Agency is to make sure that air, land and water are looked after by everyone in today's society, so that tomorrow's generations inherit a cleaner, healthier world.

This is a section of their report from April 2003.

> A study published last year by the UK Climate Impacts Programme warned that, without significant cuts in greenhouse gas concentration, the pace of climate change will quicken, with annual warming rates of between 0.1 °C and 0.5 °C a decade. That rate of change equates to between six and ten times the warming experienced during the last century.
>
> The experts predict increases in the frequency and intensity of winter flooding and summer drought, with hotter, drier summers and milder, wetter winters. The impact of changes will be most damaging in the east and south-east of England, which are also expected to suffer the storm surges and floods that will accompany rising sea levels.
>
> Environment Agency, *Environment Action*, April 2003

It's raining, it's pouring!

This is a section of a news report following the floods in Europe in 2002.

> The floods hit hardest in the Czech Republic, where 15 people died and 220 000 were evacuated. In Prague, a flood this severe would normally be expected only once every 500 years; in the south of the country it was a once-in-1000-year event and some areas received half their expected annual rainfall in just four days.
>
> Freak of nature or not, the disaster was an ominous warning of the kind of events likely to be triggered as global temperatures rise. And they could happen more often than we thought, according to Richard Betts from Britain's Hadley Centre for Climate Prediction and Research in Berkshire. He warned colleagues at the meeting that they have been underestimating the risk of future flooding.
>
> *New Scientist*, 26 April 2003

7 Visit the website of the Environment Agency to find out about their work:
www.environment-agency.gov.uk/

  a View the flood warnings in place today.

  b Click on Fun + Games and then on Climate change.

8 Find out more about global warming by visiting these websites:
www.defra.gov.uk/environment/climatechange/index.htm
www.epa.gov/globalwarming

What can we do?

The problems that global warming might bring are very worrying. There are, however, things that can be done to try to slow down the rise in temperature:

- Burn less fossil fuels
- Use renewable energy sources
- Be more energy efficient
- Put catalytic converters into cars
- Walk rather than drive
- Protect the forests.

Review

Produce a leaflet explaining what people can do to help to slow down global warming. Design the leaflet to be interesting and eye-catching, to encourage people to read it.

Chapter summary

In this chapter you have found out that:
- The greenhouse effect warms up the Earth, creating a temperature suitable for life.
- Greenhouse gases are increasing in the atmosphere and are causing global warming.
- Global warming could cause sea levels to rise, leading to more flooding and changes in the weather.
- To reduce global warming we need to reduce the levels of greenhouse gases in the atmosphere.

The need for sustainable development

Introduction

In this chapter we look at an example of the negative impact that industry can have on the natural world, and some of the major political events that followed.

- Energy is transferred between organisms in a food chain.
- Pyramids of numbers represent feeding relationships in a habitat.
- The build-up of toxins in the food chain is known as bioaccumulation.
- Sustainable development is an idea that suggests we look for techniques that help us to progress without having too much of a negative impact on the environment.

In 1968, Apollo 8 orbited the Moon and sent pictures back to Earth. For the first time, the people of the Earth could see what their own planet looked like from space, and they realised that they needed to protect the planet if they were going to survive.

This pyramid of numbers shows the number of organisms in each stage of a food chain:

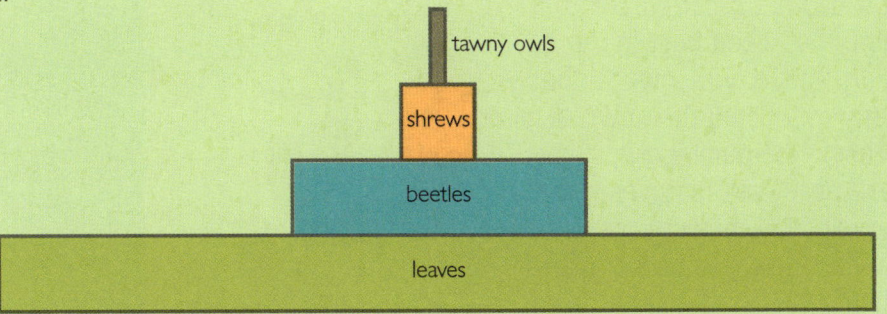

tawny owls
shrews
beetles
leaves

Draw the food chain with the arrows showing the direction of the energy flow.

81

The effects of industrial progress

Since humans first appeared, they have been developing and making progress. Two giant leaps forward happened during the agricultural and industrial revolutions. Then, when the Second World War ended in 1945, the industrial nations set about developing their countries further in order to increase their wealth and power.

The fishermen of Minamata bay in southern Japan had been selling and eating their catch for as long as anyone could remember. This included octopus, squid, sea bream and yellowtail.

In 1959 the people of Minamata started to notice a problem with the behaviour of their cats. The cats staggered and twitched before they died. Very soon, the same symptoms appeared in humans as well. Doctors from the local University filmed patients as they trembled and had shaking fits. Other people became paralysed and numb, and women began to give birth to babies that were partly paralysed, with brain damage and blindness.

The symptoms were given the name of Minamata disease, and by 1960 thousands of people were affected with over seventy dead. The doctors suspected metal poisoning and realised that it had not occurred before a PVC chemical factory had been built in the bay. The Chisso Corporation, who owned the factory, secretly conducted their own tests on the effluent they were pumping from the factory into the sea. They discovered that the two parts per billion of mercury present in their effluent was the cause of the disease. The management of Chisso did not reveal their evidence, however, believing that waste and dirt were inevitable consequences of progress. Workers at the factory claimed that if anyone spoke up about the heavy metal poisoning, they were ignored.

Tests by government scientists confirmed the connection between the disease and the presence of mercury but, because no laws were passed to prevent the pollution, Chisso continued to release the effluent into the bay for another ten years.

1. Draw a pyramid of numbers for the food chain of Minamata bay using the cartoon strip on page 83.
2. Label the producers in the food chain.
3. Label the primary consumers and the top predator.
4. What is a catalyst?

The effects of mercury on the body

Post-mortem examinations revealed high concentrations of mercury in the kidneys, liver and brain of those poisoned.

Survivors were partially or totally paralysed and had lost most forms of sensation. Many were blinded. Mothers who themselves showed no signs of poisoning bore infants who suffered from mental disability and cerebral palsy. The developing foetuses had evidently accumulated mercury from their mothers' blood.

Poison in the food chain

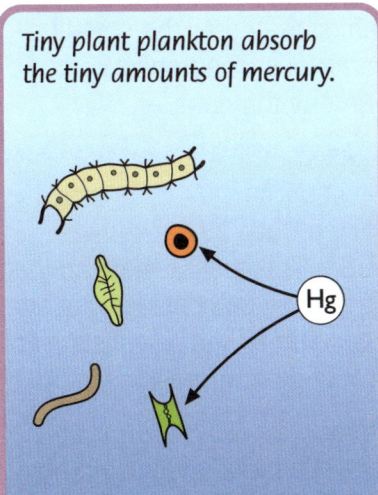

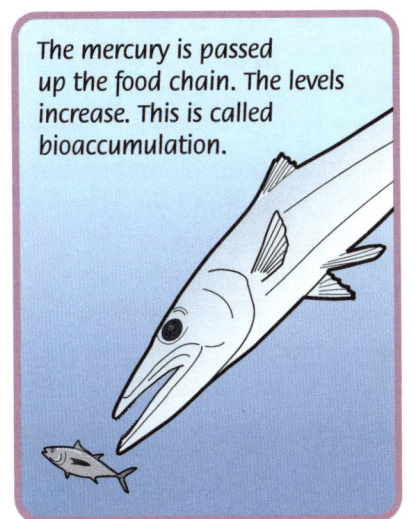

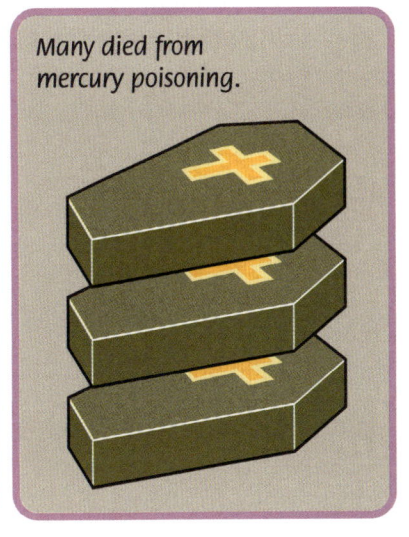

Mercury arrives at the chemical factory.

The mercury is used as a catalyst in the production of plastics.

Waste mercury is released into the water of Minamata bay.

Tiny plant plankton absorb the tiny amounts of mercury.

Zooplankton eat the plankton and the mercury levels increase in their bodies.

Mercury stays in the body so, when fish eat the zooplankton, the levels increase again.

The mercury is passed up the food chain. The levels increase. This is called bioaccumulation.

When the people of Minamata ate the fish, the mercury had reached toxic levels.

Many died from mercury poisoning.

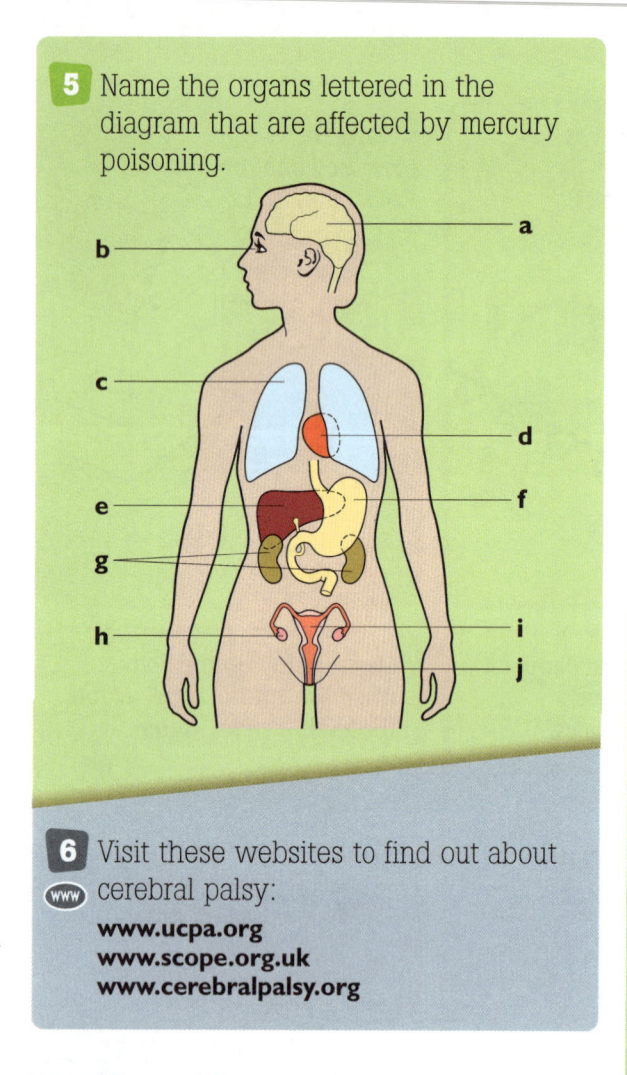

5 Name the organs lettered in the diagram that are affected by mercury poisoning.

6 Visit these websites to find out about cerebral palsy:
www.ucpa.org
www.scope.org.uk
www.cerebralpalsy.org

Paying the price

In the 1970s, the world population woke up to the devastating impact pollution, such as this, was having on our world. This spurred the victims of the Minamata tragedy into action.

They confronted the Chisso Corporation managers at a shareholders' meeting and demanded compensation. The intense public and media pressure eventually led to an apology from the president of Chisso himself. He chose the ultimate humiliation for a businessman in Japan, which is the traditional apology of bowing so low your head touches the floor.

The issue was not forgotten about even after this apology was made. In 1990, the manager of the chemical plant, Kuniyuki Takeshita, was quoted as saying: 'I do believe that without protecting nature we cannot survive. Even if profits have to suffer, the environment must come first.'

The surviving victims continue to tell their story to visiting school children, and mercury poisoning remains in Minamata bay, so fishing has not yet been resumed there.

Key environmental events that followed

1960s 'Flower Power' began in the USA and spread around the western world. Many young people demonstrated in the streets to show their concern about the impact of modern life on the environment.

1970 President Nixon (USA) created the Environment Protection Agency and passed the Clean Air Act to reduce atmospheric pollution in the USA. This meant that cars had to pass stringent tests to be considered road-worthy and manufacturers had to consider the impact of cars on the environment.

1970s Residents of Love Canal in the USA asked Government officials if they could be re-housed, but they were ignored. Their housing estates and schools had been built on the site of a burial ground for 20 000 tons of toxic waste that was leaking and causing epilepsy and asthma in the children. To gain attention and support for their plea, they took government officials hostage and locked them in the houses to see whether they appreciated having to live in such a dangerous area. This action led to the residents receiving a telephone call from the White House to inform them that they would be rehoused elsewhere.

1972 The United Nations held the first international conference on the environment in Stockholm. The event was covered by thousands of journalists from all over the world. Hearing the reports about these demonstrations from their own journalists, the people of India set up a movement that they called 'lover of trees'. They demonstrated against the logging of the forests because they realised it was causing landslides, floods and loss of wildlife.

1975 From lobbying members of parliament and demonstrations, environmentalists moved on to direct action when Greenpeace carried out their first assignment. Their aim was to get between whaling ships and the whales to prevent the destruction of these animals that had reached the brink of extinction due to over-hunting. They didn't manage to prevent the killing but their film footage was seen all over the world and led to the development of numerous other conservation societies.

Late 1970s – early 1980s Improvements started to be made with industry actually boasting about the millions they were spending on the environment and the reduction of pollution.

Mid 1980s A backlash against the environmental movement began with President Reagan (USA) and Prime Minister Thatcher (UK) claiming that the ideas were extreme and would not benefit economic growth. The evidence, however, continued to mount. For example:

- There were oil spills from tankers.
- An explosion in a chemical factory in Germany poisoned fish in the Rhine.
- An explosion at an American-owned chemical factory in Bhopal in India created a toxic gas cloud. Over 2000 people were killed outright and 20 000 blinded or disabled – the largest recorded number of people to be affected by one pollution tragedy.
- A nuclear reactor exploded at Chernobyl in the USSR (now Ukraine). Many fire-fighters were killed by radiation sickness immediately and thousands who lived nearby later died of cancer. The fall-out spread over most of Europe, and for years afterwards sheep from some areas were too radioactive to be eaten.
- The effects of acid rain were seen in Canada and Scandinavia showing that pollution was travelling from one area to another.
- A hole in the ozone layer was discovered.
- The greenhouse effect and the effects of global warming were published.

1987 The World Commission on Environment and Development, chaired by the Prime Minister of Norway, published a report called 'Our common future' that introduced the concept of sustainable development.

In the last forty years of the twentieth century, the planet lost half its rainforests, one-fifth of organisms became extinct or were threatened with extinction and countless lakes and rivers were poisoned.

---

7 Work in groups to research the effects of one of the following:
- Oil spills
- Nuclear waste and radioactivity
- Acid rain
- Chlorofluorocarbons (CFCs) and the ozone layer
- Greenhouse gases and global warming
- Litter and landfill sites

To help you with your search, try visiting:

www.bbc.co.uk/news
www.sustainable-development.gov.uk/education/
www.environment-agency.gov.uk/fun
www.globalgang.org.uk/

Produce a poster or a PowerPoint presentation so that you can present your findings to the rest of the class.

What is sustainable development?

The idea of sustainable development was first brought onto the international agenda in 1987. It is defined as development that meets the needs of the present without threatening the ability of future generations to meet their own needs.

8 Recycling waste is something we can all do to work towards sustainable development. Measure a sample of rubbish to work out how much of it could be recycled. You will need:
- plastic gloves
- bin bags
- scales
- disinfectant and cloth

This is what you do:

1 Wear the plastic gloves as you collect rubbish from around the school

2 Weigh the bin bags that you have collected and make a note of the total mass

3 Empty out the rubbish and divide it into two piles: can be recycled / can not be recycled

4 Return the recyclable rubbish into the bin bags and weigh again

5 Calculate the percentage of the total rubbish that could be recycled by using the following formula:

$$\frac{\text{mass of recyclable rubbish}}{\text{total mass of rubbish}} \times 100 = \%$$

6 Take this waste to your nearest recycling point and dispose of the rest of the rubbish in the usual way

7 Wipe down the desks with the disinfectant

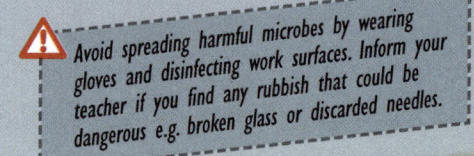

⚠️ *Avoid spreading harmful microbes by wearing gloves and disinfecting work surfaces. Inform your teacher if you find any rubbish that could be dangerous e.g. broken glass or discarded needles.*

9 What types of recycling do you normally do? Create a class list. What recycled products do you use? Compare this second list to the first.

Review

'We must continue progressing all the time so that we stay rich enough to survive.'

'We must stop using fossil fuels as they create too much pollution.'

'The people of the developing world must not be allowed to chop down their rainforests as we need the trees to give out oxygen.'

'The people of the developing world should be allowed to progress so that they can have the same standard of living as those in the west.'

'I recycle my rubbish, so I'm doing everything I can to protect the environment.'

Read these statements and work out your opinion of each one. Use your opinions to organise your thoughts on sustainable development and the problems of pollution. Have a class debate on the theme: 'Is sustainable development "too little too late"?'

Chapter summary

In this chapter you have found out that:
- The number of organisms in a food chain can be represented by a pyramid of numbers.
- Pollution can lead to the bioaccumulation of toxins in the food chain.
- Individuals and industrial corporations must act responsibly to reduce the effects of pollution on the environment.
- There is a need for sustainable development if we are to continue to progress without affecting the safety of future generations.

Life on Mars

Introduction

In this chapter, we consider whether life could exist on Mars.

- Suitable physical conditions are needed for life to exist.
- Scientists all over the world need to work together to study the physical conditions on another planet.
- Altering the physical conditions can make the whole environment more suitable for life.

Can we maintain the conditions needed for life on planet Earth? This may depend on sustainable development. Check your understanding of sustainable development by writing down what you think it means. Compare your definition with a partner. Join with another group and decide on the best description to feed back to the rest of the class.

Where did life start?

Scientists have estimated that life began on our planet 3400 million years ago.

There are some scientists who believe that life might have arrived here in the rocks that fell from space. Over millions of years, asteroids and meteorites have been colliding with the surface of all the planets in our Solar System. Bacteria inside these rocks may have brought life to this planet. This could mean that life once existed on the planet Mars, or it might be that it's just beginning.

The physical conditions on Earth have allowed life to flourish, evolving over millions of years into all its different varieties, some of which are now extinct. We have learnt about these extinct life forms from fossils. If we could find fossils on Mars we would know that life once existed there too.

Since learning about the universe, people have been fascinated about the possible existence of life elsewhere. There are many stories written about aliens, Martians being a particular favourite.

On 27 August 2003, Mars came closer to Earth than it had done for nearly 60 000 years. The last time it had been that close, Neanderthal man had been alive. It is interesting to think what they might have thought about this bright light in the night sky.

Mars.

1 The entries in the second column of the table are jumbled up. Copy the table and match each physical condition of planet Earth to the reason why it is suitable for living things.

Physical condition on Earth	Why it is suitable for life
A. Greenhouse gases in the atmosphere.	The gas needed for photosynthesis.
B. Ozone layer in the atmosphere.	The gas needed for respiration.
C. Earth's average temperature is 22°C.	Prevents harmful ultra-violet radiation reaching the Earth's surface.
D. Carbon dioxide makes up 0.04% of the air.	Trap heat so that the Earth's average temperature is 22 °C.
E. Oxygen makes up 21% of the air.	Water is in liquid form which is essential for life.

Studying Mars

Exploring space might help us to understand more about life on Earth. The first pictures of Earth from space showed us our beautiful blue planet, but also made us think about how small we are in this enormous universe and whether or not we are alone. If we could find evidence of life on other planets, it would change the way we think about everything.

The table shows a few examples of the studies of Mars that have taken place so far.

Year	Study	Discoveries
1971	Mariner 9 (USA) was the first probe to orbit Mars.	A dust storm surrounded the whole planet when Mariner 9 arrived. As the dust settled, pictures were sent back to Earth showing volcanoes bigger than any we have here. The main gases in the thin atmosphere were found to be carbon dioxide and argon, but the atmosphere had no oxygen and no ozone layer. The average temperature of the planet was recorded at −55 °C.
1976	NASA landed two Viking probes.	The probes were looking for signs of life but none were found. It was later discovered that the instruments might have been faulty, so the results of the study were not reliable.
1990s	NASA studied a meteorite from Mars.	NASA announced that they had found fossilised bacteria inside the meteorite. Scientists cannot agree, however, that the crystals are actually the fossil remains of bacteria.
1997	Mars Global Surveyor is sent into orbit around Mars.	Pictures are sent back showing fresh lava from volcanoes and what look like valleys and dried-up river beds, which means that water must have been flowing over the land.
1997	Pathfinder mission took place.	A robot buggy moved over the ground taking close-up pictures of the rocks and collecting samples for analysis.
2003	European Mars Express, and Beagle 2 (UK) launched.	The space probe Mars Express dropped off Beagle 2 into the atmosphere of Mars. It was to land and look for signs of life, for example, carbon and methane gas. The landing took place but Beagle 2 has failed to send back any messages to Earth. It must have been damaged during the landing. Just weeks after the landing, NASA successfully landed a 6-wheeled robot whose mission was to study the rocks and soil surface. Mars Express has discovered that Mars is more volcanically active than we previously thought, and the presence of ammonia it has detected in the atmosphere may be a sign that microbes are living on Mars.

> ### Life journeys
> Beagle 2 was named after HMS Beagle, which was the ship that Charles Darwin sailed on. During the voyage, Darwin visited the Galapagos Islands, which is where he found evidence to explain his theory of the evolution of life.

Scientists know that the climate on Mars is similar to the climate at the North and South Poles on Earth. The polar caps on Mars are made from frozen water and frozen carbon dioxide. In the winter on Mars, the temperature can drop to −125 °C.

These extreme physical conditions, however, do not mean that life couldn't possibly exist on Mars. On Earth, bacteria have been found living in Antarctica in temperatures well below freezing. Bacteria also survive on Earth in temperatures as high as 113 °C, in pools of acid and in areas where the radiation levels are really high.

Whether or not bacteria have once lived or are living on Mars has still to be discovered.

Does this meteorite from Mars hold fossil bacteria? It contains tiny grains of magnetite, some in the form of crystals that, on Earth, only living cells are thought to make, and every magnetite crystal in the meteorite has the same flaw, matching the flaw found in the crystals that cells on Earth make. To some scientists, this is proof that the meteorite crystals must have been produced by bacteria on Mars, but many others remain sceptical.

Preparing a second home

The increase in the size of the human population has begun to have serious effects on the physical and biological conditions of our planet. We are destroying natural habitats in order to create space for houses and for growing crops. We are polluting the air, land and sea with chemicals that are toxic to life. There is evidence that this pollution is causing the greenhouse effect, acid rain, and the destruction of the ozone layer.

Governments around the world have discussed the need for sustainable development. We need to protect our own planet to keep it suitable for life, which means reducing the pollution that we create.

But what if we can't do this? What do we do if the conditions on Earth change so much that our own survival is at risk? Would it be possible to live on another planet?

Scientists have been looking at ways of making Mars suitable for humans to live on. It is called terraforming and they think it could be done like this:

- Nuclear reactors are used to bring about chemical reactions in the atmosphere around Mars. More carbon dioxide will be produced.

- These reactions increase the greenhouse effect of the atmosphere so that the temperature of the planet rises. Bacteria can then be released that use carbon dioxide from the atmosphere and release oxygen. Other types of bacteria can change the nitrogen in the atmosphere into nitrates in the soil. Nitrates are important minerals for the growth of plants.

- 50 years later, the conditions could be suitable for planting trees. Trees would carry out photosynthesis. More oxygen would be released into the air. Some of this oxygen could change into ozone. An ozone layer in the atmosphere would protect the planet against the harmful ultra-violet radiation from the Sun.

- After 100 years, 20% of the atmosphere would be oxygen gas. The average temperature on Mars would be 15 °C. The conditions would now be suitable for human life.

It sounds very easy, but in fact it would be extremely difficult to terraform Mars. It would cost billions to do it and there are likely to be problems and setbacks at every stage.

In January 2004, however, President Bush announced that the USA would be starting a new programme of space exploration. They will be sending people to the Moon in order to set up a base. From this base they will be able to send missions to Mars. Perhaps life on Mars will exist in the future because we will create it there – only time will tell!

Web Links

Visit this website to find out more about studying Mars, and search for 'Mission to Mars': **www.bbc.co.uk/news/1/hi/sci/tech**

Review

'We should not be wasting money on trying to send people to Mars. The money would be better spent trying to protect our own planet from the damage we are causing to the natural environment. Governments should be concentrating on sustainable development, because if we can't look after Earth we won't be able to look after any other planet either.'

'I think we should be studying Mars, but just for the scientific interest. We should not try to change the planet in any way because if there is life on Mars we could destroy it by the changes we make.'

'We must look at preparing Mars as a future home. We might not be able to save Earth in the future, so we will need somewhere else to go.'

Decide which of these opinions you agree with and give a reason to explain your choice.

Chapter summary

In this chapter you have found out that:
- Scientists have sent space probes to Mars to look for signs of life.
- Life can only exist if the conditions are suitable.
- It may be possible to terraform Mars to make it suitable for humans to live on in the future.

Answers

Linnaeus and the classification system
P3 Q3
Evolution = a gradual change in the characteristics of a population from generation to generation.
Ancestor = an early type of animal or plant from which future generations have evolved.
Genes = units of inheritance; made of DNA; carried on the chromosomes.
Nucleus = control centre of the cell containing the chromosomes.

P3 Q4
Examples include the following.
Similarities: Animals with wings and eyes.
Differences: Insects are not warm blooded. Birds are covered in feathers. Bats are covered in fur. Birds have a beak. Bats have live young and feed them milk.

P3 Q5
Examples include the following.
Similarities: Plants with yellow flowers.
Differences: Dandelions spread their seeds through the air. Roses have thorns. Daffodils only appear once a year in the spring as they spend the rest of the year underground as a bulb.

P5 Q6
Bison bison = American bison/buffalo
Pan troglodytes = chimpanzee
Felis lynx = lynx/bobcat
Panthera tigris = tiger
Orcinus orca = killer whale
Canis lupis = wolf

P5 Q7
384 BC to 1758 AD = 2142 years

P6 Review

Vertebrate group	Characteristics of the group
Fish	Live in water; have scales and fins; breathe through gills.
Amphibians	Live on land but must lay their eggs in water; have a smooth, moist skin.
Reptiles	Live on land where they lay eggs with leathery shells; have dry, scaly skin.
Birds	Warm blooded and lay eggs with hard shells; have feathers, wings and a beak.
Mammals	Warm blooded; covered in fur/hair; give birth to live young and feed them on milk produced in mammary glands.

Superorganism
P7 Introduction
Invertebrates

P7 Q1
Diagrams should show bees taking the pollen from the anthers of one flower to the stigma of a flower from another plant.

P8 Q2
Queen has larger abdomen because her function in the hive is to lay all the eggs.
Drone has large eyes as he needs to be able to see well for flying.
Drone has hairs on abdomen for heat insulation.

P8 Q3
50 000 − (1 + 250) = 49 749

P9 Q4

Structure of the worker bee body	How it is adapted to carry out its functions
Pollen combs on the front legs	Shaped so that they can scrape through the fur to remove the pollen
Spikes on the middle legs	Shaped so that they can scoop wax from the wax gland or pollen from the baskets
Back legs	Hairy and strong for carrying the pollen baskets
Stings and venom sac	To attack other animals in order to defend the hive
Tongue	Long tube for sucking up nectar
Mandibles	Shaped for chewing and biting
Intestine	Contains a sac for storing the nectar being taken back to the hive

P11 Q5
Pupate = When an insect is changing from a larva to an adult, e.g. caterpillar to butterfly.

P11 Q6
d Bacteria, fungi and viruses all spread infections.

P11 Q8
Enzyme = molecule that can speed up a chemical reaction without being used up itself.

P11 Q9
8000 × 25 = 200 000

P12 Q10
The bee's dance shows: whether the food is towards or away from the Sun; the angle between the food and the Sun; the distance of the food from the hive; a sample of what the food tastes like.

Forensic entomologists
P14 Introduction
One possible solution: The person is locked in the cellar, the river floods its banks, the cellar fills up with water, the person drowns, the water drains away again.

P15 Q1
Invertebrate animal = animal without a backbone.

P15 Q2
(a) blowfly, (b) wasp, (c) termite, (d) ant, (e) beetle

P16 Q3
a Herbivore = an animal that eats plants.
b Carnivore = an animal that eats meat; may be a predator or may feed on dead meat (carrion).
c Omnivore = an animal that eats both plants and other animals.

P16 Q4
1024

P16 Q5
Egg → Maggot → Pupa → Fly
P18 Q8
Maggots grow fastest when temperature is highest.

Sharks – the profile of a predator
P19 Introduction
Plankton (Producer) → Small fish (Primary consumer) → Large fish (Secondary consumer) → Dolphin → Shark → Man (Top predator)
P21 Q1
Examples include the following.
Similarities: Gills for breathing; have a skeleton.
Differences: Skeleton of cartilage instead of bone; no flap covering the gill slits; skin of denticles instead of scales; no swim bladder; most give birth to live young instead of laying eggs.
P21 Q4
2 × 48 = 96
P23 Q6
Oil is less dense than water, so the mass of 1 cm^3 of oil is less than the mass of 1 cm^3 of water. Water molecules are packed more closely together than oil molecules.
P24 Q8
Diagrams should show the particles in a liquid closer together than the particles of a gas, making it easier/faster for sound energy to be passed from one vibrating particle to another.
P26 Q11
On horizontal axis: Species of shark, in the following order: Hammerhead, Thresher, Great White, Tiger, Blue, Mako.
PP26/27 Review
Across: 3, 7 = protective oceanic device, 9 = adapted, 10 = finning, 11 = pectoral, 12, 14 = whale shark, 13 = sensory.
Down: 1 = dorsal, 2 = streamlined, 4 = cartilaginous, 5 = mermaid's purse, 6 = elasmobranchs, 8 = carnivores.

Behaviour of wild animals
P30 Q1

Technique for studying behaviour	Advantages	Disadvantages
Controlled experiments in the lab	The direct relationship between an independent and a dependent variable can be investigated by carrying out a fair test.	Wild animals may not behave naturally in artificial conditions, so the results may not be accurate or reliable.
Observations in the wild	Wild animals are more likely to be behaving naturally.	There are too many variables that can't be controlled, so it is not a fair test. Time-consuming.

P31 Q4
a Light or dark conditions.
b The behaviour of a sample will be more representative of the population of woodlice than just one woodlouse.
c Area of the choice chamber for each condition should be the same size; all the woodlice should enter the choice chamber in the centre, 5 minutes between each time to count; same species of woodlouse.
d All woodlice then have an equal choice about which section of the choice chamber to go to.
f Increase the sample size by repeating with other woodlice; extend the time of the experiment so that more measurements can be taken.
P35 Q7
a For comparison; to see how quickly a sample of people could solve the maze without any positive or negative external influences.
i The behaviour of a sample will be more representative of the population than of just one person.
j Increase the sample size by repeating with other people of various ages etc.

Responding to the seasons
P37 Introduction

Season	Physical conditions	Biological conditions
Spring	Warm temperature, increased light levels.	Spring flowers grow from bulbs, trees in blossom, new leaves in bud, lambs born.
Summer	Hottest temperatures of the year, longest hours of daylight, least rainfall.	Increase in insect populations, summer migrants, e.g. swallows arrive, flowers and plants grow quickly.
Autumn	Temperature and light levels start to decrease, rainfall increases.	Fruits and berries produced, deciduous trees start to lose their leaves, insects die out or go into hibernation, summer birds migrate.
Winter	Lowest temperatures of the year, shortest hours of daylight, increased rainfall and risk of snow and ice.	Conifers maintain foliage all year round, animals hibernating or have thick winter coats.

P40 Q6
a Bag 1 = dried leaves in the lab; Bag 2 = wet leaves in the lab; Bag 3 = leaf litter in the lab; Bag 4 = leaf litter in low temperature; Bag 5 = leaf litter in the light; Bag 6 = leaf litter in high temperature.
b Equal mass of leaf litter; equal area of material to make net bag; all bags secured with elastic bands; each bag left for the same amount of time.
c Whether each bag is getting the same types of leaves in the leaf litter that have all fallen from the same tree at the same time; whether there are any decomposer organisms mixed in with the leaf litter; the number and type of decomposer organisms.

P41 Review
a What is meant by biological conditions?
b What is germination?
c Why do deciduous trees lose their leaves before the winter?
d How do hibernating animals insulate themselves from heat loss?
e What is migration?

Animal adaptations
P43 Q1

Habitat	Physical conditions
Desert	Very high temperatures during the day, low temperatures at night; shortage of water
The ground of a British woodland	Damp; low light levels – dappled light through the canopy; cool temperature.
The canopy of a tropical rainforest	Hot and humid; dappled but bright light.
Arctic Ocean	Temperature and light levels decreasing with increasing depth; salty water.

P43 Q2
Producer → Primary consumer → Secondary consumer → Top predator

P44 Q3
Owl has sharp talons to grasp prey animals and tear flesh. Duck has webbed feet to increase the surface area for pushing itself through the water. Blackbird has thin toes pointing in different directions that can easily wrap around thin branches, so that the bird keeps out of the way of predators, such as cats.

P44 Q4
Compared with the red fox, the Arctic fox has smaller ears to reduce surface area for heat loss; thicker fur covering more parts of the body for increased insulation.

Peppered moths
P49 Introduction
Order: Consider the present scientific evidence; Use data already collected to help develop a hypothesis; Test the hypothesis; Analyse the data; Draw conclusions from the data; Evaluate the conclusion and compare with previous scientific evidence.

P52 Q2
a $123/447 \times 100 = 27.5\%$
b black, black, pale, 13, 27.5
c Pale variety: $62/496 \times 100 = 12.5\%$;
Black variety: $30/473 \times 100 = 6.3\%$.
d In the non-polluted area, a greater proportion of the pale variety was recaptured because it was better camouflaged from birds. The birds could see the black variety much more easily on the pale trees, so fed on them and reduced their numbers. Only 6.3% of those released were recaptured compared to 12.5% of the pale variety.

P52 Q3
Possible reasons might be:

a Kettlewell could compare the number of moths released with the numbers that survived and were caught again.
b Kettlewell could check that birds were actually feeding on the moths and could see directly if the variety of moth made a difference to how easily they were captured. These observations provided further evidence, helping to make his results more reliable.
c Kettlewell needed time to breed the moth populations he required.
d With the numbers of each variety very similar, Kettlewell could make more direct comparisons, helping to make his results more reliable.

Lichens and air pollution
P54 Introduction
Describe... → Plan... → Keep... → Present... → Analyse... → Come... → Evaluate...

P56 Q2
... stays fairly constant.

P56 Q3
To make comparisons between the growth of lichens before the road was built and after.

P57 Q5
a There was a decrease in the growth of lichens; the nearer the road, the greater the decrease.
b Mechanical equipment and works traffic during road building would have released gases that polluted the air, e.g. SO_2. This air pollution could have killed the lichens growing on the trees in the woodland.

P57 Q6
One year later the percentage cover of lichens on the trees was still at a very low level compared to before the road was built. However, there was a small increase in numbers furthest from the road, perhaps indicating that the air pollution had reduced slightly or dissipated (i.e. spread out, therefore reducing its impact).

P57 Q7
Two years later, a small recovery in the growth of lichens continued. Over the two years since road building, at 91 m from the road there was an increase in lichen coverage of 6% compared to zero increase at 1 m. Five years after building, however, there was an increase at every sampling position along the transect. The greatest increase was again furthest from the road: a 16% increase at 91 m compared to a 1% increase at 1 m.

P57 Q8
All the results show a decrease in the percentage cover of lichens when the road was being built and, every year afterwards there was a direct relationship between the percentage cover and distance from the road, i.e. as the distance from the road increases the percentage cover of lichens increases.

P57 Q9
Reasons might include: Reduction in the amount of traffic compared to the building year; air pollution dissipated; car/fuel design may have improved, with less SO_2 released in exhaust fumes.

P57 Q10
No: percentages may continue to increase but are unlikely to reach the levels before the road was built.

P57 Q11
More samples could be taken along this transect; increase the number of transects in this woodland; repeat the experiment in a similar situation so that the data can be compared.

Extinctions
P59 Introduction
600 million years ago (Precambrian) → 440 million years ago (Ordovician) → 350 million years ago (Devonian) → 270 million years ago (Carboniferous) → 135 million years ago (Jurassic) → 70 million years ago (Cretaceous) → Today (Quaternary)

P60 Q1
Definition of a chemical element: **b**

P60 Q2
deoxyribonucleic acid

P60 Q3
3397 000 000 years

P60 Q4
a Temperature, rainfall, light levels, wind speed/direction, speed/direction of ocean currents etc.
b Volcanic eruptions, earthquakes, meteor impacts, floods, hurricanes etc.

P62 Q6
65m years ago – 3m years ago = 62m years

P62 Q7
a Calculated from the quantity of iridium.
b Test the rocks that were laid down during this time: look for iridium or volcanic dust.
c Asteroid = small (max. 670 km diameter) planetoid that moves around the Sun mainly between the orbits of Mars and Jupiter. Comet = a body of frozen material that orbits the Sun in an ellipse; when it gets close to the Sun, part of it defrosts and vaporises, leaving a trail behind it.
d Photosynthesis
e Sulphur dioxide (SO_2)
f To protect themselves from being eaten by herbivores.

Fish farming
P66 Q1
a Plankton
b Make their own food by photosynthesis.

P66 Q2
Reasons might include: farming provides abundant food supplies, improved hygiene and medical care reduces the number of deaths by disease.

P66 Q3
What happens at an extinction: **c**

P67 Q5
1000 kg = 1 tonne

P67 Q7
Pie chart with: 29% = 104.4° from fish farms; 71% = 255.6° from the sea.

P68 Q9
Gills

P68 Q10
Vaccinations prevent disease and antibiotics cure disease.

P68 Q11
Pyramid starts with highest bar at base for algae; decreasing bars for shrimp, cod and humans.

GM crops
P71 Q3
a Roots
b Produce their own food by photosynthesis and this energy is available for all the other organisms in the food chain.

P71 Q4
Best to describe organic farming: **c**

Pesticides versus biological control
P72 Starter
Pests: Slugs, Foxes, Locusts, Rabbits, Greenfly, Rats.
These can be pests if they feed on crops: Elephants, Cows and Goats.

P73 Q2
a Method of pest control; pesticide or biological control.
b Yield of tomatoes.

P74 Q3
For comparison; to compare the yield of the tomatoes when no pest control method has been used with when it has.

P74 Q4
reliable

P74 Q5

Fair test point	Why it needs to be kept constant	Possible effect on the results if not kept constant
Tomato variety	Different varieties grow at different rates to a range of different sizes.	The yield will depend on the variety as well as on the method of pest control.
Age of tomato plants	The plants produce their tomatoes after a certain amount of growth.	Yield will depend on the age of the plant as well as the method of pest control.
Type of compost used	Different types contain different amounts of minerals.	Minerals affect the growth of plants which will affect the yield of tomatoes.
Mass of compost	Different amounts of compost will contain different amounts of minerals.	Minerals affect the growth of plants which will affect the yield of tomatoes.
Volume of water	Water is needed for photosynthesis. The volume of water will affect how quickly the plants make glucose.	The faster a plant can photo-synthesise, the greater the yield is likely to be.

(Continued overleaf)

Fair test point	Why it needs to be kept constant	Possible effect on the results if not kept constant
Time when the plants are watered	Water needs to be available to all the plants at the same time so that all the plants are experiencing the same conditions as each other.	Plants that are not given water at the same time may not have an equal opportunity to use the water for photosynthesis, therefore reducing the amount of glucose produced. The yield of tomatoes will consequently be lower than for other plants.
Greenhouse temperature	Temperature affects how quickly a plant can carry out photosynthesis.	The faster a plant can photosynthesise, the greater the yield is likely to be.
Amount of sunlight	Sunlight provides the energy that a plant needs to carry out photosynthesis.	Plants with more light can carry out more photosynthesis. They will grow faster and this will increase the yield of tomatoes.

P74 Q6

Measurement	Apparatus	Units
mass	balance/scales	kg/g
volume	measuring cylinder	l/cm³/ml
time	stopwatch	min/s
temperature	thermometer	°C
amount of sunlight	light meter	lux

P74 Q7
Examples: Size of pots the plants grow in; percentage CO_2 in greenhouse air; position of pots in each greenhouse – shelf heights/at greenhouse centre or at sides.

Global warming and flooding
P76 Introduction
CO_2 0.04%; N 78%; other gases 0.96%; O 21%
P77 Q1
carbon + oxygen → carbon dioxide
P77 Q2
300 °C
P77 Q4
a For a fair test.
b For comparison.
c Heat energy dissipates from water into air.
d Should slope down to the right.
e Graph for control results should slope down much more steeply than for the insulated flask.
f Should reduce the heat loss by insulating the flask.
P78 Q5
Coal, oil, natural gas.
P78 Q6
water; oxygen

The need for sustainable development
P81 Introduction
leaves → beetles → shrews → tawny owls
P82 Q1
Pyramid starting with largest bar at base for plant plankton, decreasing bars for zooplankton, small fish, large fish, humans
P82 Q2
Producers = plant plankton
P82 Q3
Primary consumers = zooplankton; top predators = humans
P82 Q4
Catalyst = a substance that increases the rate of a chemical reaction without itself being used in the process.
P84 Q5
a brain; b eyes; e liver; g kidneys

Life on Mars
P89 Q1
A. Trap heat so that the Earth's average temperature is 22°C.
B. Prevents harmful ultra-violet radiation reaching the Earth's surface.
C. Water is in liquid form which is essential for life.
D. The gas needed for photosynthesis.
E. The gas needed for respiration.

Index and glossary

page

9 **abdomen** the 'belly' of an animal's body

63 **abuse** to misuse

54 **accurate data** precise measurements/results and without error

90 **acid rain** rainwater that is more acidic than natural rainwater

9 **adaptation** (**adapt**) any change in the structure or function of an organism that makes it better suited to its environment

63 **advent** arrival

55 **algae** (singular: **alga**) simple plants that live in very moist places; do not have true stems, leaves or roots

49 **analyse** examine in detail to find relationships or patterns

68 **antibiotics** medicines produced by microbes that destroy bacteria

33 **associate** link or connect together

88 **asteroids** small rocky objects that orbit the Sun

84 **asthma** a disease where people find it difficult to breathe

15, 39, 88 **bacteria** single-celled micro-organisms

46 **binocular vision** seeing with both eyes

40 **breathing rate** speed of breathing in and out

24 **buoy** a floating object that is anchored to the bottom of the sea; boats can moor to it or navigate by it

43 **canopy** the highest level of branches and foliage in a forest

80 **catalytic converter** a device on a car that removes the harmful gases from the exhaust fumes by changing them into less harmful gases before they enter the air

49, 54 **conclusion** a final decision based on results; description of the relationship between the independent and dependent variables

16 **confessed** admitted to be true

54 **constant** fixed, unchanging, the same

30 **contract** get smaller in size

32 **court** attempt to mate with

89 **crystals** solid substances with regular shapes and definite angles

49 **data** observations or measurements

63 **decades** periods of ten years

40 **decay** rot away

40 **decomposed** broken down by bacteria and fungi; rotted; decayed

32 **defend** protect from harm or danger

22 **dense** tightly packed (as for particles)

20 **denticles** small tooth-like parts, e.g. the scales of sharks

38, 70, 78 **drought** a long time without rain

46 **duped** tricked

82 **effluent** liquid discharged as waste from sewage works, industrial plants and factories

63 **enforce** make sure people obey the law

84 **epilepsy** a disorder of the central nervous system in which people lose consciousness from time to time

38 **Equator** an imaginary line round the middle of the Earth

57 **eroded** wear away

17, 67 **estimate** make a rough calculation

79 **evacuated** withdrawn from a place of danger

49, 54 **evaluate** judge the value or worth; consider how firm the conclusions of an investigation can be

17, 49 **evidence** data collected and analysed

2 **excretion** discharging waste from the body

44 **expanding** increasing in size

57, 66 **extinct** condition when all the organisms of a particular species have died out

10 **fertilised** when the nuclei of male and female sex cells have joined together

69 **fertiliser** a natural or artificial mixture of minerals that increase plant growth when added to the soil or water

15 **food chain** represents the transfer of energy from the producer to consumers; each animal eats the organism below it in the chain

26 **food web** combination of food chains in a habitat where there is overlap of organisms

52, 78 **fossil fuels** fuels formed over millions of years from the remains of dead organisms

88 **fossils** remains of dead plants and animals that have been made into rock

9 **function** the job carried out by a particular structure

39 **fungi** (singular: **fungus**) simple plants that do not contain chlorophyll

9 **glands** cells or organs in the body that make and secrete chemical substances

29 **habitat** the place where an organism lives that has particular physical features

40 **heart rate** the speed the heart beats and pumps blood around the body

44 **herd** a large group of mammals living and feeding together

64 **hydroelectric dam** a barrier holding water in a reservoir until it is allowed to fall; the moving water generates electricity when it moves a turbine

49 **hypothesis** a suggested explanation

14 **identification/identify** recognising something

50 **industrial** linked with industry, i.e. manufacture or construction

10 **infection** disease passed from one person to another

29 **infra-red** radiation; heat

23 **instinctive** describes built-in responses of an animal to particular stimuli

28 **interact** act closely with each other

54 **interpret** explain the meaning of results from an experiment

60 **invertebrates** animals without a backbone

54 **lichens** simple plants formed from an alga and a fungus

16, 39 **life cycle** the series of changes occurring in the life of an organism

5 **memoirs** a collection of memories from your life

88 **meteorites** rock-like objects that are the remains of meteors that have fallen to Earth

29 **migrating** populations of animals moving to an area where the conditions are more suitable for survival

15, 69 **minerals** natural nutrients/chemicals needed for health, obtained from the soil by plants

59 **molecules** chemicals consisting of two or more atoms joined together

60 **molluscs** invertebrate animals that often have a shell

41 **navigate** travel following particular directions

88 **Neanderthal man** a type of primitive man from late Palaeolithic times

9 **nectar** Sugary liquid produced by flowers

30 **nervous system** brain and nerve cells in the body that carry information

46 **nocturnal** relating to the night

32 **nurtured** supported during development

67 **nutritious** nourishing; providing the nutrients for life and growth

29 **offspring** children

79 **ominous** describes a danger

21 **orbit** the path a planet or satellite travels

26 **over-fishing** catching more fish than can be replaced by reproduction

85, 89 **ozone layer** a layer in the atmosphere that absorbs ultra-violet light

47, 82 **paralysed** unable to move

39 **photosynthesis** the method plants use to make their own food from carbon dioxide and water, using light energy from the Sun

15, 43 **physical conditions** the non-living conditions in a habitat

23 **plankton** tiny plants or animals that live in the surface layer of the sea

9, 70 **pollen** male sex cells produced in the anthers of flowering plants

7, 70 **pollinate** transfer pollen from the anthers to a stigma

54 **pollutant** a substance that causes pollution

26 **pollution** contamination by poisons or harmful substances

49 **population** a group of organisms of the same species living in a particular area

23 **pores** small openings

19 **predator** an animal that hunts, kills and eats other animals

40 **prediction** decision made in advance of the likely outcome of an experiment using your knowledge of similar or related events

44 **prey** an animal hunted or captured by another animal for food

18 **primary consumer** an animal that eats the producers in a food chain

18	**producer** a plant at the start of a food chain that can make its own food by photosynthesis		2	**stimuli** things that cause a response
82	**PVC** polyvinyl chloride; plastic		8	**structures** the parts of the body and how they are organised
68	**pyramid of numbers** a diagram showing the numbers of organisms at each level of a food chain		38	**sufficient data** enough results have been measured to identify any patterns in the data
63	**quotas** the shares or parts of a whole allocated to one person or group		40	**surface area** the area of the exterior faces of an object
85	**radioactive** describes a substance that releases radiation		82	**symptoms** any changes in the function of the body because of a particular disease
32	**rampage** rush about in an angry or violent way		28	**termite** whitish social insect that often feeds on wood
10	**regurgitating** bringing partly digested food back into the mouth		32	**territory** an area that an animal or group of animals defends as its own
54	**reliable data** results of a test or experiment that can be used to make a firm conclusion; the more evidence that there is in favour of a particular result, the more reliable it is		48	**tertiary consumers** animals that feed on the secondary consumers in a food chain
80	**renewable energy sources** those resources that provide energy and will not run out during the Earth's lifetime		62	**theory** a set of ideas to explain and predict a wide range of phenomena
2	**reproduction** how organisms have offspring		19	**top predator** the animal at the end of the food chain
69	**resistant** to fight against		84	**toxic** poisonous
2, 89	**respiration** a chemical reaction that uses oxygen to release energy from food		89	**ultra-violet radiation** radiation from the Sun that has a shorter wavelength than light but longer than X-rays
30	**retina** the light-sensitive layer at the back of the eye		30	**unconscious** not aware of what is happening
51	**rural** of the countryside		32	**unprecedented** not having happened before
31	**sample** a small group that represents a population		68	**vaccinated** treated with a vaccine against a particular disease to bring about artificial immunity
24	**scavenge** feed on decaying matter		9	**venom** a poisonous fluid secreted by some animals
10	**scent** a smell		30	**vertebrate** animal with a backbone
18	**secondary consumer** an animal that eats the primary consumers in a food chain		23	**vibrations** rapid movements back and forth
39	**seed dispersal** the method by which seeds are spread from a parent plant		41	**water vapour** water in the gas state
32	**skin graft** a piece of skin removed from one part of the body and surgically grafted at the site of an injury			
23	**snout** the nose and jaws of an animal			
7	**social** describes living in a community			
50	**soot** carbon from the burning of coal or wood			
13	**sperm** male sex cell			
39	**starch** carbohydrate made from a chain of glucose molecules			
46	**stationary** not moving			

Acknowledgements

The publishers would like to thank the following for permission to use copyright material. Every effort has been made to trace copyright holders and to obtain their permission for the use of copyright material. The author and publishers will gladly receive information enabling them to rectify any error or omission in subsequent editions.

Text:

p.5 *Dragons* taken from *Life on Air* ©David Attenborough, BBC Publications; p.29 *Beyond Innocence*, Reprinted by permission of Sll/Sterling Lord Literistic, Inc ©Dale Peterson; p.32 *Rampaging badger puts five people in hospital* by Sam Lister ©The Times/NI Syndication; p.63 *Fall in fish stocks hits crisis point* by Ian Sample and *Extinction stares 25 species in the face* by Alok Jha ©The Guardian; p.64 *Birds found–then habitat destroyed* ©New Scientist; p.79 *Time to 'climate-proof' England and Wales* ©Environment Agency. p.79 *Here comes the rain* © New Scientist.

Photographs:

p.24 ©James D Watt/Stephen Frink Collection/Alamy; p.25 bottom left ©Ron and Valerie Taylor/Stephen Frink Collection/Alamy, top right ©Jeff Rotman/Alamy; p.29 ©Steve Bloom Images/Alamy; p.45 top©Claudia Adams/Alamy, bottom ©Michael & Patricia Fogden/Corbis; p.50 ©Michael W. Tweedie/Science Photo Library; p.51 ©Michael W. Tweedie/Science Photo Library; p.55 ©Dr Jeremy Burgess/Science Photo Library; p.81 ©NASA/Science Photo Library; p.88 ©NASA/Roger Ressmeyer/Corbis; p.90 ©NASA/Science Photo Library